CARE FOR CREATION

Care
for
Creation

[a franciscan spirituality of the earth]

ILIA DELIO, O.S.F.
KEITH DOUGLASS WARNER, O.F.M.
PAMELA WOOD

FOREWORD BY DENIS EDWARDS

Franciscan
MEDIA
Cincinnati, Ohio

Excerpts from *Francis of Assisi: Early Documents,* volumes 1, 2, and 3 edited by
Regis J. Armstrong, J.A. Wayne Hellmann and William J. Short, copyright ©1999
reprinted with permission of New City Press.

The Keeling Curve is reprinted with permission of the artist Robert A. Rohde
of Global Warming Art, www.globalwarmingart.com.

Scripture passages have been taken from *New Revised Standard Version Bible,* copyright ©1989
by the Division of Christian Education of the National Council of the Churches of Christ in
the U.S.A., and used by permission. All rights reserved.

Cover design by Sandy L. Digman
Cover image © www.istockphoto.com/Emrah Turudu
Book design by Mark Sullivan

LIBRARY OF CONGRESS CATALOGING-IN-PUBLICATION DATA

Delio, Ilia.
Care for creation : a franciscan spirituality of the earth / Ilia Delio, Keith Douglass
Warner, Pamela Wood ; foreword by Denis Edwards
p. cm.
Includes bibliographical references and index.
ISBN 978-0-86716-838-9 (pbk. : alk. paper) 1. Nature—Religious aspects—
Christianity. 2. Human ecology—Religious aspects—Christianity. 3. Creation. 4.
Franciscans. 5. Spirituality—Catholic Church. I. Warner, Keith. II. Wood, Pamela. III.
Title.

BT695.5.D3785 2007
261.8'8—dc22

2007048883

ISBN: 978-0-86716-838-9
Copyright ©2008, Ilia Delio, Keith Douglass Warner and Pamela Wood. All rights reserved.

Published by Franciscan Media
28 W. Liberty St.
Cincinnati, OH 45202
www.FranciscanMedia.org

Printed in the United States of America.
This book is printed on recycled paper.
16 17 5

For our Franciscan sisters and brothers—
those who have gone before us,
those who are with us
and those who will follow

"THE HUMAN COMMUNITY AND THE NATURAL WORLD
WILL GO INTO THE FUTURE AS A SINGLE SACRED COMMUNITY
OR WE WILL BOTH PERISH IN THE DESERT."

—Thomas Berry

[contents]

•

•

•

[foreword]

Earth, with all its creatures, is in crisis, and responding to this crisis will require every possible resource of our human community. One of the most precious of these resources is the Franciscan tradition. It is a joy to welcome this book as a wise, thoughtful, inspiring and practical contribution to ecological theology, grounded in the ancient Christian tradition that sees the Earth as our sister and mother. *Care for Creation* is part of a wider retrieval of Franciscan theology for our new time, but it is unique in its blend of three interrelated disciplines: scientifically informed ecology, theology and the practice of reflective action.

Reading this manuscript led me to reflect on how my own theological journey has been informed and shaped by the tradition of Francis and Clare. It is not only that Francis has been my companion, with his image hanging over my desk for many years as I have worked on ecological theology. It is also three fundamental lines of thought that have shaped my own thinking that have sprung from this Franciscan tradition. The first is the kinship of creation, the theological insight that we (all of God's creation) are all fellow creatures, each uniquely loved and valued by God. This means, of course, that we cannot treat any of our fellow creatures as if they exist without value. In spite of all the distinctions between us, we are family. In my view both kinship and the call "to till and keep" creation (Genesis 2:15) are fundamental in locating the human vocation within the wider creation before God. But the heart of ecological conversion is the invitation to see, feel and act in this kinship of creation.

A second theological insight from the Franciscan tradition was mediated to me long ago through the work of the great Jesuit theologian Karl Rahner. Rahner follows the Franciscan theologian John Duns Scotus in holding that God creates a universe of creatures with the Incarnation in mind. The Incarnation does not come about simply as a result of sin. It is not a second, remedial step—although it certainly brings us forgiveness. God always intended to give God's self to us in the Incarnation and take us to God's self in the final consummation of all things. God's one act of self-bestowal has the distinct dimensions of creation and Incarnation. In my experience of teaching, I have discovered that most Christians do not have access to this theological position and feel relief and joy in discovering it. And, as this book makes clear, this insight from Scotus, along with other Franciscan thinkers, provides the basis for linking ecology and Christology at a radical level.

The third great learning for me occurred about sixteen years ago while I was on study leave at the Center for Theology and the Natural Sciences at Berkeley. As well as learning about science and theology, I found myself spending months reading Bonaventure and discovering in his Trinitarian theology abundant resources for an ecological theology that takes Christology and the Trinity as central. For Bonaventure ecstasy and fecundity are located at the heart of the Trinity. The dynamic goodness of the Fountain Fullness (the *fontalis plenitudo*) finds expression in the eternal Wisdom and Word, the Exemplar, and reaches its loving culmination in the Spirit. With the free choice to create, what this Trinitarian dynamism comes to is fruitful expression in an interrelated world of diverse creatures. Every creature is a work of art of the Trinity. Every organism, every species, every ecosystem is the self-expression of the dynamic Trinitarian life, a sign of the divine presence. The biotic community of a rain forest, a wetland or a household garden is the work of art of divine Wisdom.

These three insights are dealt with in rich detail in the pages that follow, along with a great deal more, and the whole contributes beautifully to the theory and the practice of ecological conversion. At the heart of this book is a profound conviction that responding to the Incarnation, the Word made flesh, commits us to the interrelated world of flesh, to the biological community of Earth. Resisting ecological conversion is, theologically, resistance to the Incarnation. To be truly ecologically converted to Earth in a fully theologically sense will involve a conversion to the Incarnation.

—*Denis Edwards*

Most High, all-powerful, good Lord,
Yours are *the praises, the glory* and *the honor* and all *blessing,*
To You alone, Most High, do they belong,
and no human is worthy to mention Your name.
Praised be You, my *Lord,* with all *Your creatures,*
especially Sir Brother Sun,
Who is the day and through whom You give us light.
And he is beautiful and radiant with great splendor;
and bears a likeness of You, Most High One.
Praised be You, my Lord, through Sister *Moon* and *the stars,*
in heaven You formed them clear and precious and beautiful.
Praised be You, my Lord, through Brother Wind,
and through the air, cloudy and serene, and every kind of weather,
through whom You give sustenance to Your creatures.
Praised be You, my Lord, through Sister *Water,*
who is very useful and humble and precious and chaste.
Praised be You, my Lord, through Brother *Fire,*
through whom *You light the night,*
and he is beautiful and playful and robust and strong.
Praised be You my Lord, through our Sister Mother *Earth,*
who sustains and governs us,
and who produces various *fruit* with colored flowers and *herbs.*

Praised be You, my Lord, through those who give pardon for Your love,
and bear infirmity and tribulation.
Blessed are those who endure in peace
for by You, Most High, shall they be crowned.

Praised be You, my Lord, through our Sister Bodily Death,
from whom no one living can escape.
Woe to those who die in mortal sin.

Blessed are those whom death will find in Your most holy will,
  for *the second death* shall do them no harm.
Praise and *bless* my *Lord* and give Him thanks
  and serve Him with great humility.[1]

NOTE

[1] Francis of Assisi, "The Canticle of Creatures" in *Francis of Assisi: Early Documents*, vol. 1, *The Saint*, Regis J. Armstrong, J.A. Wayne Hellmann and William J. Short, eds. (New York: New City, 1999), pp. 113–114. Hereafter referred to as *FA:ED*, vol. 1, 2, or 3 and followed by page number.

[introduction]

A number of years ago, Thomas Berry, one of the most prominent voices in ecotheology, was pleading ardently that more attention be paid to our environmental situation. In his talk he suggested that we put the Bible aside and stop using the name of Christ explicitly. He indicated that our Western Christology had obscured the primacy of the Earth as a book of revelation. "We are in the midst of the greatest change of humankind," he said, and he warned us of impending doom if we do not radically change our approach to development. According to Berry, spirituality is concerned with conversion, and in an ecological age it calls for a deeper awareness of the horrendous damage humans have inflicted on the earth. Even though Christianity is a creation-centered religion, we have turned our attention away from the earth and toward heaven in hope to gain eternal life.

It seemed odd at the time that Berry, a Catholic priest, wanted to suspend explicit talk of Jesus Christ for the sake of the Earth. After all, as Christians should we not be public about whom we claim to follow? He made it seem that institutionalized Christianity was an obstacle to caring for the Earth, and, although at the time this idea seemed scandalous, Berry had a point. Something had gone awry in Christianity. We Christians not only profess belief in a personal creator, God, but we say that creation is good and God has loved it to perfection by entering into it, taking on human flesh and dwelling with us as the risen Christ. Yet our environmental crises are the most ominous threats facing humanity. How do we Christians proclaim the alleluia of the risen Christ while the garment of our natural world is being rent from top to bottom? Something, indeed, is amiss.

FRANCIS: PATRON SAINT OF ECOLOGY

In 1979 Pope John Paul II named Saint Francis of Assisi the patron saint
of those who promote ecology because he recognized the importance
of his God-centered life for our modern age.[1] He gave formal recognition to the popular perception of Francis' relationship with nature as
ecologically ideal. Saints are models of holiness worthy of studying and
following. Saints can help shape us into the disciples we desire to be.
Francis is one such saint, perhaps the most popular saint of all time. His
universal appeal lies in his simplicity of heart, his dedication to the following of Christ, his love of the poor and his fellowship with all creatures. He loved creation passionately, as a brother, lover and friend of all
living beings. But what does it mean for us to have a patron saint of ecology? What implication does this model Christian hold for people of faith
everywhere who are concerned about the future of our planet? First,
Francis recognized God's work in creation and loved it. He was foremost
a follower of Jesus, but in him there was no tension between loving God
and loving all creatures of God. Rather, Francis reveled in the sun, gazed
upon the stars, danced with the air, was drawn to the fire, marveled at
water and loved the earth. He recognized the beauty of God in creation
and loved God all the more for the abundance of this gift. Although he
predated modern scientific conventions, he celebrated the beauty and
interdependence of creation through poetry and called it "good." Francis
recognized the interdependence of human beings with one another and
with the rest of creation. Second, Francis experienced God in creation,
and this is a most helpful starting point for contemporary Christian theology. He preached about his experience in such a way that Franciscans
have continued to emphasize the importance of creation as "God-
centered" throughout our theological tradition. Francis' emphasis on
"God as good" inspired prominent Franciscan theologians such as
Bonaventure and John Duns Scotus, who spoke of creation as the revelation of God's overflowing love. Third, Francis provides an example of
reflective action. He encountered the pain of the world, which inspired

him to pray, but also to act with compassion and to proclaim gospel values. Because contemporary Franciscan spirituality carries forward this tradition, a book addressing these three dimensions of Francis' approach to the environment is long overdue. This book's format is designed to integrate these three approaches: ecology, theology and reflective action.

•

ENVIRONMENTAL CRISIS AND THE WORD OF GOD

There are a number of reasons why we find ourselves in an environmental crisis: technological, cultural and economic revolutions. But for Christians the crisis may be even more fundamental. Christians are in a crisis of the Word of God. We Christians have no real grasp of the living Word of God. Jesus was a good person, but do we believe that he is the Christ, the living Word of God who dwells in our midst? Many seem to believe in God not because the living Word of God interrupts our daily lives on Earth but because it is better to believe than not to believe. We do not know what awaits us after death, and the promise of heaven and eternal life seems worthwhile for an act of faith. As a result, creation is not our primary concern. We may hope for a new heaven and a new *Earth* but we don't really believe such hope has anything to do with *this Earth*.

The crisis of the Word is a crisis of *theology*—literally—"God talk." We have lost a Christian theology that adequately conveys the idea that creation is God speaking to us. However, this is indeed what the Franciscan theologian Bonaventure claimed. The first book of revelation, he said, was the "Book of Creation." Before sin entered the hearts of humans, we could read this book intelligently and know God through the things of creation. However, once sin entered into the human condition, the "Book of Creation" became unintelligible, like a foreign language to us. Only one like Francis, who lived a life of conversion, could read the "Book of Creation" and understand its meaning. The "Book of Creation" spoke to Francis in such a way Bonaventure said that "In beautiful things, he contuited Beauty itself."[2] Thomas of Celano wrote that "He walked reverently over rocks, out of respect for Him who is called *the Rock*."[3] The meaning of creation would be lost to us forever, Bonaventure indicates, if Christ had not come and enlightened the darkness of the human heart. Christ is *the* Book of Life through whom we can learn to read once again the "Book of Creation." Because sin has rendered creation like a closed book, we are given the Scriptures to know God and the things of God. Reading, understanding and contemplating the Word of God leads us back to creation as the revelation of God.

Language mediates or discloses being to us. Language is said to take on the character of an event when it "sets something in motion," when it transcends the boundaries of a mere statement and becomes an address.[4] In oral cultures words were living things. In the early church those who went out to the desert to live the gospel life lived in profound silence so that when words were spoken they could be readily received as actions in their lives. For the desert fathers the Word of God carried authority and burst forth in "events" of revelatory power. Word events transformed their lives.[5] The power of the Word changed, however, when the Word became a printed Word and thus a "thing" out there on a flat surface. Walter Ong suggested that such "things" are not actions but are in a radical sense dead, though subject to dynamic resurrection.[6] Through the technology of the printed word, the power of the spoken word lost its power to change lives. The word as a living *thou* confronting a living *I* became a dead-letter *it* in the printed word, only to become a *thou* according to interpretation of the reader. The development of the printed word changed the nature of personal encounter, and we might speculate that the printed word was our first rift with nature. The early Franciscans such as Francis and Bonaventure lived during an oral and written culture. Although Bonaventure was a university-trained theologian and knew how to read and write Latin, still he was immersed in a primarily oral culture that relied on listening and attentiveness to words that were spoken. It is not surprising therefore, that Bonaventure spoke of creation as a "book." By this metaphor he indicated that one did not have to be educated or trained in theology to know God. One simply had to be attentive to the beauty, goodness and order of creation to know that God has revealed himself to us in love.

Reading requires good eyesight; it is a matter of vision that leads to understanding and insight. Eyesight and insight belong together. The more clearly we can see, the more deeply we can know, and the more deeply we know, the more we touch the ground of truth. The contemporary theologian John Haught has suggested that we need a new "vision" to move us to a firm and permanent commitment to ecological responsibility within the context of natural flux and cosmic evolution.[7] This new vision, he indicated, corresponds to the need for a new identity and insight, a "more animating and far-reaching articulation of what it means to be Christian in an ecological age."[8] Such an identity, however, must be nurtured by a new and more profound relationship with God, and an understanding of the Word of God, as that Word comes to us in the person of Jesus Christ. How do we reclaim the Word of God as a living Word, a Word that impacts our lives daily, changes us, moves us in a direction as pilgrims of the Earth? How do we come to read the Book of Creation as the "words" of God's overflowing love? How can creation speak to us once again of God?

Francis of Assisi is a model of a person changed by the living Word of God. His official biographer, Bonaventure, described Francis as one who heard the Word of God and put it into practice. The Word was not a dead letter for Francis but the living Word of life. In one of the early chapters of his biography, Bonaventure describes how Francis was attending Mass one day and devoutly heard the Gospel being read in which Christ sends out his disciples to preach and gives them the gospel form of life. "Hearing, understanding, and committing this to memory," Bonaventure wrote, Francis exclaimed, "This is what I want...this is what I desire with all my heart. Immediately, *he took off his shoes from his feet,* put down his staff, denounced his wallet and money, and, satisfied with one tunic, threw away *his leather belt* and put on a piece of rope for a belt." Then Bonaventure adds, "He directed all his heart's desire to carry out what he had heard and to conform in every way to the rule of right living given to the apostles."[9] Francis of Assisi became a lover of the Word. Although he was especially attuned to hearing the Word of God through the reading of the Scriptures, Francis knew the Scriptures to be the living Word of God, and this Word pulled him into the current of created living beings. Francis found God in the cloister of creation. His love and understanding of the Incarnation, the Word made flesh, grew by touching, tasting and seeing the good things of creation.

In his book *At Home in the Cosmos*, David Toolan dubbed Francis a "biocentrist" because Francis found God in the sun, the moon and stars, flowers, trees and even wild wolves.[10] For some modern scholars, such piety may be a bit like "sap," but Francis' life was not a saccharine euphoria. His was a difficult life because he allowed the Word of God to change him. Francis did not simply hear the Word and walk away as if it were never spoken (which is quite common in our time). From the beginning of his conversion, when he encountered the Word of God in the crucified Christ, Francis heard God speak to him in the depths of his heart and he remained attentive to that voice of the living Word throughout his life. Living in the Word of God impelled Francis to follow the footprints of Christ because he saw those footprints imprinted on his soul, on the hands of a leper and on the fragile creatures of creation. Francis believed that God walked in creation in the person of Jesus, and he continued to follow God's footprints by following Christ so that he could climb up and embrace his beloved. Francis provides for us an example of an engaged spirituality.

•

FRANCIS IN OUR TIME

We would be remiss, however, to superimpose Francis' life onto our own age, as if eight centuries had not passed. He lived in a very different cosmos than our own, a medieval cosmos marked by hierarchy, fixed order, perfection and anthropocentrism (the belief that humans are the most significant entities in the universe). Earth was the center of the cosmos, and the human was center of the Earth. Following the description of the cosmos by the Greek astronomer Ptolemaeus, it was believed that Earth was surrounded by seven spheres carrying the planets, which greatly influenced birth, death and all phenomena on in the sublunary world. As center of the cosmos, Earth was immovable. Above the spheres of the planets there were higher spheres, the lowest of which carried the fixed stars. The whole cosmos was completely round and the planets moved in a circular orbit. The macrocosm (the cosmos itself) and the microcosm (the human person) were perfectly attuned to each other and constructed according to the same basic plan and, indeed, contained the same basic elements. In a word, the whole cosmos had been perfectly arranged by the Creator.[11] Bonaventure wrote that "The First Principle made this sensible world in order to make itself known, so that the world might serve as a footprint and a mirror to lead humankind to love and praise God, its Maker."[12] Although we live in a different cosmos than Francis, a dynamic, expanding, evolutionary universe, the purpose of creation for us is the same as it was for Francis and Bonaventure, to lead us to "love and praise God, its Maker." Does this creation lead us to "love and praise God"? Do we confront creation as a sacred book? If so, why are the pages torn and the imprints of God's words erased?

Environmental problems are religious crises because at their core, they are crises of meaning. Human society, therefore, appears incapable of responding to these problems without addressing the questions of human consciousness and our moral vision. In 1990 a group of leading scientists called on religious communities to play a more active role in addressing our environmental problems, including especially their religious and ethical dimensions.[13] They suggested that we are committing "crimes against creation." This statement provoked a 1991 summit of religious leaders to formulate an interfaith response to the current environmental crisis. Denominations of many religions have subsequently issued statements on the environment. In the United States leaders of Jewish, Catholic and Protestant denominations launched the National Religious Partnership for the Environment, which is now the leading voice on the interface of ecology and religion. In the mid-1990s Harvard University hosted a series of major international meetings on religion and ecology and launched the Forum on Religion and Ecology.

Although many religious groups have become increasingly aware of their responsibility to the environment, still there is a lag in—if not out-right resistance to—ecological conversion among many Christians. It is within this context that a Franciscan spirituality of the Earth finds its voice, since it is a spirituality that takes as its starting point the Incarnation, that is, God united with human nature and, hence, with creation. Although there have been scholarly works on a Franciscan theology of the environment,[14] this is the first book to articulate a Franciscan spirituality of creation that includes environmental studies, Franciscan theology and faith formation. It draws on the renewed interest in the Franciscan movement in our intellectual tradition, and its potential to contribute to contemporary challenges.[15] The gravity of our situation is such that we need a new "turn to the Earth," but we will not turn unless we understand at a theological level why such a turn or conversion is necessary. Unless the mind understands through insight, the heart will not be moved to change and thus to love. Fanning the flames of love has long been intrinsic to Franciscan theology, and reflective action can help us creatively engage with the needs of the world.

•

WHAT TO EXPECT FROM THIS BOOK

This book is divided into four principal sections, each of which contributes toward the development of a Franciscan spirituality of creation. The first part describes the relationship between the Earth as God's creation and Jesus as the Incarnation of God. The Franciscan tradition has always insisted on perceiving creation and Incarnation to be fully and integrally related. The second part examines the implications of Francis'

"Canticle of Creation" for our time. It describes the diversity of life, analyzes the biodiversity and extinction crises and raises troubling questions about how and why humans are tearing at the fabric of life. The third part examines the role of contemplative prayer in creation in light of global climate change. This is the most fundamental environmental challenge facing the future of life on Earth. We believe contemplation to be a spiritual practice essential to our Franciscan tradition, and key to discovering Francis' awe and respect for creation. The final part examines conversion in the Franciscan tradition. Human society is on the brink of another transformation: the sustainability revolution. Here again Francis can inspire us to care for creation, because for him, conversion was an occasion for joy, an opportunity to respond to God's activity in the world with the same generosity. This is the kind of spiritual practice Christians desperately need to recover.

Each of the four parts is comprised of three chapters: one each on ecology, theology and reflective action. Applied ecology, or environmental studies, provides a critical lens for understanding human interdependence upon Earth's ecosystems, and an appropriate tool for interpreting our contemporary environmental crises. The first chapter of each part, therefore, will discuss a key application of ecology to our environmental problems. The second chapter of each part will take up the ecological topic at hand from the point of Franciscan theology, drawing from the life of Francis, the writings of Clare and the theology of Bonaventure and Scotus. The purpose of articulating theology is to provide an understanding of the God-world relationship and the place of humans within God's good creation. In the third chapter of each part, we offer reflective action opportunities designed to bring our ecological and theological insights into your daily life and nurture a Franciscan spirituality of the Earth. It offers prayers, meditations, spiritual practices and group activities that provide practical, hands-on approaches to reconnecting with the Earth and acting in right relationship. We believe that this format will help facilitate a deep learning about our environmental problems and provide resources to offer nourishment for spiritual formation and, on a larger scale, cultural transformation. The three appendixes provide additional resources, including a guide for using the reflective action sections of the book to cultivate an ecological consciousness and spirituality for each of us and our communities, and a select bibliography for further learning about care for creation in the Franciscan tradition.

Francis offers us an example of an engaged spirituality, and if we let his life transform our hearts, we will naturally be inspired to take action to restore justice in our world. The ecology-theology-reflective action format of this book will provide rich opportunities for integrating the principles of ecology and theology through a whole-person faith formation process both on an individual level and communal level, engaging your faith community and the larger society. The ecological devastation of our time can often feel so overwhelming and our power to impact it so insignificant; thus, we also believe that it is crucial to discuss the barriers that keep us from an ecological conversion of heart and from taking action to heal our world. Reflective action sections include actions and practices that can help us become more aware of—and overcome—what keeps us from taking action. Please take the time to work with the reflective action sections so that you can fully integrate the concepts of this book into your own life.

The past four decades of environmental crises have taught us that knowledge of the crises alone does not necessarily result in any change in attitude or behavior. Unless we can begin to "think with the heart," we will not be moved to change our attitudes and behaviors toward the nonhuman created world. Just as Francis learned to read the Word and put it into action, we, too, must find a way to see creation as the mirror of God, even in its perilous condition. Our prayer is that this little book may help you undertake a journey of personal and community transformation so that an abundance of life may flourish on this planet Earth.

NOTES

[1] Pope Paul II, "S. Franciscus Assisiensis Caelestis Patronus Oecologicae Cultorum Eligitur," *Acta Apostolica Sedis* 71 (1979). The expression "patron saint of those who promote ecology" requires some interpretation. In Europe during the 1970s, many people used the terms "ecology" and "environmental concern" interchangeably. In the U.S. we now distinguish between ecology as a scientific discipline and environmentalism as valuing the natural world and advocating for it. It appears Pope John Paul II was speaking in the European context.

[2] Bonaventure, "The Major Legend of Saint Francis," 9.1, in *FA:ED*, vol. 2, p. 596.

[3] Thomas of Celano, "The Remembrance of the Desire of a Soul" 124, in *FA:ED* vol. 2, p. 354.

[4] Douglas Burton-Christie, *The Word in the Desert* (New York: Oxford University Press, 1993), p. 18.

[5] Burton-Christie, p. 19.

[6] Walter Ong, *Orality and Literacy: The Technologizing of the Word* (London: Methuen, 1982), pp. 32–33.

[7] John Haught, "Theology and Ecology in an Unfinished Universe," in *Franciscans and Creation: What Is Our Responsibility?*, Elise Saggau, ed. (St. Bonaventure, N.Y.: Franciscan Institute, 2003), p. 1.

[8] Haught, p. 6.

[9] Bonaventure, "Major Legend of Saint Francis," 3.1, in *FA:ED*, vol. 2, p. 542.

[10] David Toolan, *At Home in the Cosmos* (Maryknoll, N.Y.: Orbis, 2003), p. 37.

[11] N. Max Wildier, *The Theologian and and His Universe: Theology and Cosmology from the Middle Ages to the Present* (New York: Seabury, 1981), p. 38.

[12] Bonaventure, *Breviloquium*, vol. 9, Robert J. Karris, ed. (St. Bonaventure, N.Y.: Franciscan Institute, 2005), 2.1.1.

[13] See frontispiece in John E. Carroll and Keith Warner, O.F.M., eds. *Ecology and Religion: Scientists Speak* (Quincy, Ill.: Franciscan, 1998).

[14] See Ilia Delio, O.S.F., *A Franciscan View of Creation* (St. Bonaventure: Franciscan Institute, 2003), *Franciscans and Creation: What Is Our Responsibility?* Elise Saggau, ed. (St. Bonaventure, N.Y.: Franciscan Institute, 2003), *Franciscan Theology of the Environment: An Introductory Reader*, Dawn Nothwehr, ed. (Quincy, Ill.: Franciscan, 2003).

[15] The Franciscan Intellectual Tradition was renewed in 2001 by the English-speaking conference of the Order of Friars Minor, which established a commission to coordinate a network of publications and initiatives. This Commission for the Retrieval of the Franciscan Intellectual Tradition (CFIT) decided that one of its first major tasks would be to identify the central themes and emphases of the Franciscan intellectual tradition, particularly as that was embodied in key theological issues. The Commission also recognized that the tradition is rich in insights as to how the Christian message might intersect with the fields of politics, economics, psychology, sociology and environmental studies. In this broader context, the present work contributes to the retrieval of the Franciscan intellectual tradition.

•

•

•

•

•

part one

CREATION
AND
INCARNATION

[chapter one]

ECOLOGY AND CREATION

Life is amazing. All life is utterly dependent upon our planet for everything it needs. God provides everything through creation. Water falls from the sky and runs through creeks and rivers. Plants and animals grow and are all part of the circle of life. Air circulates around the globe, refreshing and renewing all of life's creatures. The sun, trees, plants, oil, coal and gas provide energy. The beauty of creation grabs our attention, inspiring us and providing for our needs. God truly cares for us like a mother cares for her children and expresses this care through the goodness of creation. Our planetary home is not ours alone, however, for we live in community with an abundance of creatures upon which we depend daily, even though we rarely think about them. This chapter introduces the basic principles of the life sciences—ecology and biology—to lay the groundwork for a contemporary Franciscan care for creation. It begins by describing some of the special traits of our home planet that make it a suitable place for us (and for the Incarnation) to dwell. It then traces the role that the science of ecology can play in helping us to understand creation.

•

LIFE DEPENDS UPON THE PLANET EARTH

In our solar system, only Earth provides the conditions necessary for life. Our home planet is just close enough to the sun to allow its energy to heat our planet, but far enough away that it does not burn us. If its orbit were farther from the sun, we would live on a planet covered with snow and ice, but if it orbited closer, Earth would be too hot and survival would not be possible. All life depends on energy, and most life on Earth as we know it depends on the sun as the ultimate source of energy.[1] Solar energy reaching Earth's surface is captured by plants and converted to sugars, which in turn become the basic building blocks for life. These compounds serve as food for the other creatures. Life is only possible with food and energy, and these have their ultimate origin in the sun.[2]

•

OUR BLUE PLANET

We live on a blue planet, rich in water. Although it is but a simple two-element chemical compound, water is absolutely essential for life. Over seventy percent of our human bodies are composed of water and over seventy percent of our planet is covered with oceans. Healthy human bodies can live for many days without food, but can survive less than three days without water. According to biologists, ocean waters offer just the right conditions for the evolution of life. Ocean water with the simple molecules dissolved in it provided most of the raw material for the first bacteria, the cellular building blocks from which more complex life forms evolved. The components of the water we carry in our bodies and our tissues, the water that is the basis of our blood, once swirled in the ocean, was evaporated up into the atmosphere, and fell as precipitation. Every living creature depends on water to live, yet water hardly ever stays put. It falls from the sky, runs down to rivers and groundwater and returns to the sea.[3]

Our home planet is refreshed by life-giving air. The original chemical compounds of Earth's atmosphere were released when the planet was forming, and then the atmosphere stabilized as a mixture of nitrogen and oxygen, plus small amounts of other gases. This atmosphere nourishes and protects us. It allows the passage of solar energy, but filters out deadly rays and buffers the temperature extremes that occur on other planets. The sun heats different parts of our planet at different rates, generating wind and weather. As water evaporates from oceans and lakes, many impurities dissolved within the water are left behind, and the purified water is redistributed around the globe. No other planet offers such hospitality for life as we know it. Other planets have atmospheres of deadly gases or simply do not have a sufficiently formed atmosphere to host life.

•

OUR GREEN PLANET

We live on a green planet, rich with life. It is covered with plants and animals, and other forms of life we rarely think of. Much of Earth's land surface is blanketed by a living mantle of vegetation, which hosts animal creatures of every kind. The planet's hospitality becomes even clearer when we recognize that the entire animal kingdom depends totally on plants, whether directly or indirectly. The plant kingdom converts solar energy into a form of energy directly usable by living organisms, as water and carbon dioxide are combined to form simple sugars through photosynthesis.[4] The sugars from photosynthesis provide the energy source for plants as they assemble the materials needed to build up their roots, stems and leaves. Life would not be possible without plants and their role in converting solar energy into food through photosynthesis. Life continues so long as an unbroken flow of energy and food flows through our ecological communities.

•

OUR VIBRANT PLANET

We live on a vibrant planet, diverse in life. Insects are the most populous animal group and most of them eat the complex sugars generated by the plants. A small fraction of animals are carnivores and eat other animals (most of which have eaten plants that have converted sunlight). Because these creatures are related through their feeding habits, scientists refer to this network as a *food web*. Indeed, the food and the energy that plants provide feed the entire system of life. But a whole other, less visible, food web connects the "waste" from these creatures, whether animal excrement or dead plants and animals. Microscopic creatures, such as bacteria and fungi, spring into action to break these raw materials down into the raw materials that plants use to make their roots, stems and leaves. Life on Earth is an endless, rhythmic cycle of building up and breaking down. The plant kingdom converts solar energy and very simple molecules into stored energy, which is consumed by successive levels of animals. After all of these die, yet another group of creatures consumes them, and then this food cascades down through another food web, and the rhythm of life pulses on. This description is highly simplified, but it helps us to recognize that life is dynamic, relational and interdependent.

•

Our Home Planet

Our home planet has been reshaped by human ingenuity, science and technology. Science and technology provide benefits, but frequently they are put into practice by people who fail to recognize the impact they will have on the natural world. Many of these changes have benefited us humans at the expense of other creatures. Over the past 150 years the life (biological) sciences, especially ecology, have investigated the origins of life and relationships that sustain it. Life scientists help us understand how humans depend upon the Earth's life but also how we are harming it. Many of us perceive scientists to be unusual people conducting mysterious experiments to determine abstract truths, but at a fundamental level most scientific work is a process of observing the world, asking good questions about these observations and then checking and measuring the observations in order to answer the questions and then make some conclusions about our world. Today more than ever, we need to listen to what scientists are telling us about the human impact on nature.

•

The Study of Ecology

Biologists investigate life on Earth. The studies of Charles Darwin sparked a biological revolution in the 1860s. His theory of natural selection provided an overarching explanation for how the diversity of life has developed over time. Ecology is the study of how organisms interact

24

with one another and their environment. Rather than look for tensions and disagreements between science and religion, the Franciscan way asserts that all of us can benefit from understanding what biology tells us about life, regardless of how much or how little we understand of science. The dynamism of the whole created world is like a biological dance in which every living creature participates in interactions with other organisms and with their environment.

The root *eco-* comes from the Greek word *oikos* and is an element of the words *ecology, economy* and *ecumenical. Oikos* means "house," so these three words mean, respectively, "study of the house," "management of the house" and "universal house." Ecology became a popular term during the 1960s, as society began to recognize that we live on a planet of finite resources. Rachel Carson wrote *Silent Spring* about the environmental impact of pesticides and the fundamental interrelatedness of life. As astronauts snapped awesome pictures of our planet from space, newspaper headlines described a litany of environmental problems and the finite character of the Earth and its inhabitants. These events began to provoke new consciousness among many North Americans, most of whom had assumed that natural resources would always be abundant. Many believed that even if local resources were exhausted, more could be found just over the horizon. Popular awareness of ecology inspired some to realize that American society had split apart ecological and economic well-being, despite their overlapping meanings. The myth of infinite resources slowly began to give way to a new realization: We live in a finite system.

The science of ecology has contributed a most important concept: the ecosystem. Although few people have resisted this idea (at least relative to the resistance over the concept of evolution), the ecosystem concept is no less revolutionary. An ecosystem is an association of organisms and their physical environment, interconnected by the circulation of energy and nutrients. An ecosystem may be any size, from a drop of water to our entire planet. All creatures live within some kind of ecosystem and relate or influence each other—and their environment—by their behavior. The idea of an ecosystem is critical to understanding the patterns of life on Earth. The ecosystems' living and nonliving interactions take place on our home—Earth—and thus the connection between the idea of ecology and house (*oikos*). Different kinds of organisms meet their needs in their own unique ways, but they all need a community of other living organisms in order to live. Within an ecosystem there are three general categories of living creatures: producers, consumers and decomposers. Let us now turn to how these main components of ecosystems relate to each other in our home—the home that God created.

Producers

In Earth's ecosystem plants are the primary producers. As mentioned earlier, they convert solar energy to carbohydrates and thus make useable forms of energy for other components of their ecosystems. Except in tropical forests, most plants require soil to anchor themselves to the Earth.[5] The sun provides energy for members of the plant kingdom, soil provides them a home, and plants in turn provide the biochemical energy and building blocks of life for other creatures.

Consumers

Members of the animal kingdom are "consumers," and most of them depend on the producers for food. Herbivores, or plant-eating animals, have developed strategies to consume every kind of plant and every plant part for food: roots, stems, leaves and seeds. The majority of these consumers are insects hosted by the plants, who provide them food, moisture and shelter. Some insect consumers may live their entire lives in trees. A smaller number of consumers are carnivores, meaning they eat other animals. Most of these eat insects, but a few larger, attention-getting animals (hawks, tigers, bears) eat other large animals. Consumers also depend upon the producers to offer them protection and shelter.

Decomposers

The decomposers are just as important, yet their work is largely invisible to us. Most of their work is done shielded from our view, hidden in the soil and water. Bacteria and fungi, as well as some soil- and wood-dwelling insects, take the waste and remains of the other creatures and break them down into nutrients that are needed by plants. Healthy soil provides a home for the decomposers. They are able to reproduce rapidly when their food is abundant and die back when there is less. Decomposers then leave nutrients in the soil, in a sense converting "waste" into nutrients taken up by other organisms, especially plants. Without healthy soil, excess nutrients would run from the soil into rivers and oceans, causing pollution and other problems. Without decomposers, our planet would pile up with waste.

•

CIRCLE OF LIFE

Life would not be possible without the movement of energy and nutrients, first converted from solar energy by the plants, and then moving through food webs as consumers eat, and then back to energy through the action of decomposers. Between each stage of a food chain roughly ten percent of the energy and nutrients are passed to the consumer. Life is not linear; it is cyclical. Energy and food are moved through producers and consumers, and then back around, a cycle as continuous as our own breathing and heartbeat.[6] Energy and food in ecosystems make life possible.

Yet the interactions in this biological dance of life are not only external to humans. It also takes place within our very bodies, indeed all bodies. Our bodies are organized into specialized cells, which are in turn arranged into the tissues and organs that compose our bodies. These cells need energy to function. Food for humans originates in energy from the sun, powering photosynthesis and the creation of plant carbohydrates, which we consume directly or indirectly through animals. When we eat, our bodies produce energy through the digestive process of breaking food down into smaller units that can be absorbed, and then circulated through our body and used as an energy source within our cells. This food and energy transfer is called *metabolism*. Energy released by metabolism within cells can then be used for the many types of work that happen within our bodies, such as cellular reproduction, the building of proteins, the production of tissues that make up organs and a host of other functions that occur at the molecular level. Plant metabolism directly uses the carbohydrate products of photosynthesis to build their own plant cells and organize them into tissues and organs. Our bodies function in many ways similar to ecosystems. Energy enters our bodies in the form of food. We are home to hundreds of billions of cells, all of which work together to keep our bodies healthy and alive. They operate without any conscious effort on our part, and yet, if these cells in various organs become sick or injured, our life is imperiled. These cells, and the tissues and organs they constitute, regulate our temperature, distribute food energy, fight off diseases and sense the surrounding environment of which we are a part.

Our bodies are systems, akin to ecosystems, because they host hundreds of bacteria and fungi, and indeed, we depend on some of these creatures for our health. They help us create vitamins and fight harmful infections. The most well-known bacteria is *Escherichia coli*, which assists in digestion. Even though microscopic, this creature moves, feeds, reproduces and even seems to communicate with its own kind. If laid end to end, the *Escherichia coli* in your digestive system would reach from San Francisco to Boston.[7] When new harmful microscopic creatures, whether viruses, bacteria or fungi, enter our body, they can reproduce and harm our bodily functions. Healthy bodies respond with immune systems that help us to resist infection and disease, but sometimes the "invaders" can overwhelm our natural bodily defenses. People without strong immune systems are less able to defend themselves. Even though the organisms that cause us health problems are natural in their origin,

28

when they overwhelm our innate ability to maintain balance, we become ill, and suffer.

•

TECHNOLOGY AND THE CIRCLE OF LIFE

Today we are changing creation as never before through various technologies. The scientific revolution has given us the technological tools to extract energy and food from our planetary home at an unprecedented rate. Oil, coal and natural gas deposits were laid down within the Earth millions of years ago as plant tissues trapped by geological processes. These ancient carbon sources were fixed by the same process of photosynthesis which benefits us today. We are extracting this fossil fuel far faster than nature deposited it. Burning fossil fuel releases this energy, which we put to productive use. However, fossil fuels also release carbon dioxide and water as well as other chemicals, some of which are hazardous and form smog. Carbon dioxide in small quantities does not disturb the balance of the ecosystem. Until recently, carbon dioxide was understood to be harmless. However, recent evidence of global climate change has forced scientists to reevaluate their previous understanding of the global effects that large amounts of carbon dioxide (commonly referred to as a "greenhouse" gas) can play. (More on this in chapter seven.)

While thousands of years ago humans relied completely on hunting and gathering for food (and therefore did little to disturb the Earth), the dawn of tools, industry and technology transformed the way humans obtain food. The birth of farming and agriculture added a social dimension to the way we draw food from the Earth. Energy and nutrients from the Earth flow from farms through factories and stores to our homes and tables. Daily we depend on the fruit of the Earth and the work of human hands. The industrialization of agriculture has freed most Americans from having to work the land. Farm work is very hard work, and our lives are more comfortable as a result. Yet our farming ancestors had an intimate relationship with the Earth through their work. They depended upon the elements and seasons, plants and animals, and the cycles of life. In some ways our modern lives are easier, but has not this distancing from agriculture contributed to our alienation from creation?[8]

•

Unintended Impacts

Some agricultural technologies have had serious unintended impacts on creation. Through her book *Silent Spring* Rachel Carson brought environmental consequences of toxic pesticides to our attention.[9] Hazardous pesticides continue to be used, but this is merely the most obvious environmental problem caused by industrial agriculture. Other industrial practices threatening agricultural resources include the erosion of topsoil, the contamination of groundwater and the nutrient pollution in our lakes, streams, rivers and coasts. These do not grab headlines in the same way that toxic pesticides do, but they threaten the health of our planet, and the ability of future generations to feed themselves. Industrial agriculture has abandoned many traditional farming practices based upon ecology, such as crop rotations and using farm animals to recycle surplus crops into valuable fertilizer (manure). Concentrated agriculture feeding operations have converted animals into machines, consuming corn farmed with massive amounts of fossil fuel. Fertilizers and pesticides are manufactured from oil and gas, and Earth has but a finite amount of these. Topsoil around the world is eroding away, threatening the ability of future generations to farm. Quality soil is essential for agriculture, and by extension, human society.

It takes centuries to form just an inch of topsoil, with microbes and microorganisms working to break down rock and combine it with decaying material. Imagine a tomato 250 feet across, with a skin no thicker than an ordinary tomato: that is the average proportionate thickness of topsoil on the Earth, or at least the thirty-five percent of the Earth that is land! We are losing topsoil to wind and water erosion far faster than it can be replaced. Agriculture requires water, and in many parts of the world irrigation systems are taking water from rivers and streams and harming aquatic life. Industrial agriculture consumes water from underground aquifers far faster than it can be recharged. Future generations will have less soil, fossil fuels and clean water than we do. Sadly, much of this is due to the manner in which our resources are wasted, used inefficiently or simply managed without reverence for their Creator.

Carson revealed a most disturbing irony: The industrial agriculture producing the food upon which we all depend is threatening the ecological basis for life. She argued that we could not continue to disregard the consequences of human industrial agriculture without serious, long-term consequences. Agriculture was by no means the only activity causing these problems. Nuclear weapons, war, fossil-fuel burning, industry and our consumer society are all, to some extent, responsible. Yet her message applied to much of modern industrial society: If we do not change our ways, future generations will awake to silent springs. Human activities are responsible for driving many species to extinction and fraying the fabric of life. More recent studies have shown that hundreds of the harmful industrial chemicals she warned about have entered our bodies through the air we breathe, the water we drink and the food we eat. These toxic chemicals are so ubiquitous that they are found in most human breast milk. They may be responsible for many diseases, but providing scientific proof of this is very difficult.[10]

Carson's insights laid the foundation for the emergence of the concept of *sustainability*. This term rose to popularity in 1987 with the United Nations (UN) report entitled *Our Common Future*. Also known as the Brundtland Report, it defined sustainability as meeting the needs of the present without compromising the ability of future generations to meet their needs.[11] The emergence of sustainability marks a conceptual breakthrough for human society because it reconnects economic well-being with the ecosystems that compose our planetary *oikos*. A slow realization across the globe is developing. The *oikos* depends upon our care, upon humans practicing restraint, upon humans translating their care for creation into environmental protection. As we can see from Figure 1, human society is only one subset of the environment, and the economy is a subset of that. For example, agriculture constitutes one of the essential relationships between humans and the Earth. We gather resources (nutrients) from the environment, and through the labor of society, we feed the economy, which produces goods we like, but also creates waste, which we do not want. This figure indicates a profound yet easily overlooked truth: We live in a finite world, and we and our economy are inextricably dependent upon the well-being of creation. Other than solar energy, Earth has a finite amount of resources. The practical implications of Franciscan care for creation today means helping human society become more sustainable.

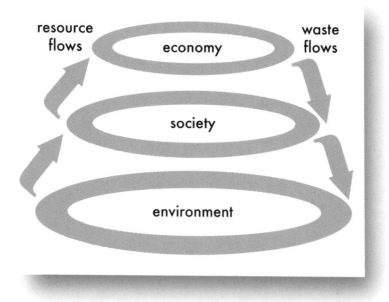

Figure 1. Our economy is situated within society, which is situated within the natural environment and its resources.

A FUNDAMENTAL LESSON

A fundamental lesson to learn from ecology and an understanding of ecosystems is that every resource we need comes from somewhere, and everything we throw away goes somewhere else. Figure 1 also illustrates how human society returns waste to the environment. For most of history, human resource use and waste deposition had a negligible impact on the Earth. With human population now more than twenty times what it was during the time of Francis of Assisi, and the rate of consumption far greater, we are shredding the fabric of life and dumping more waste than the Earth can absorb. The consumer societies of North America, Europe, China and Japan are the greatest threat to the sustainability of our planet. We who live in affluent countries have the power to make alternative choices, to curb our consumption and live lives of greater simplicity, motivated by our care for the Earth.

•

OUR ECOLOGICAL FOOTPRINT

Williams Rees and Mathis Wackernagel have developed the idea of an ecological footprint to measure the impact of consumption and waste on the earth.[12] This is a simple tool that can help us perceive our impact on the earth by measuring resources we use (directly and indirectly), and the planet's ability to absorb waste products. They determined the amount of area it takes to grow food and fiber, to mine minerals and fossil fuels and to dispose of our trash. The ecological footprint lets us measure the impact that our individual and social choices have on creation. Part four of this book will discuss how to use this tool to minimize our impact and contribute to sustainability. All human beings consume resources and leave an impact. Having needs is part of being human. We all leave behind some kind of mark, some signs. Francis sought to follow in the footprints of Jesus. Note that he did not use the term *footsteps,* but *footprints.* Francis understood the Incarnate Lord of history to have left visible signs in which he could follow. Creation became the material home for the Incarnation during Jesus' life on Earth. Creation was

capable of holding Jesus' body, and Jesus left footprints for us to follow. How can this Franciscan insight help us with our spiritual journeys today?

•

Conclusion

The fundamental task for a contemporary Franciscan spirituality of creation is to translate our care for the natural world into concrete initiatives to reduce our individual and social impact on the Earth. The life
sciences provide contemporary followers of Jesus helpful and important
insights into creation, how it is organized and how its components relate.
The science of ecology can offer everyone insight into how organisms
interact with one another and their environment, and thus how our
home planet is host to life. Science helps us recognize the beauty, diversity and fecundity of our planetary home. It helps us to perceive the
interdependence of all life, yet by itself, science cannot teach us to care,
nor to recognize creation as the most suitable home for the Incarnation.
Something deeper is needed, something that reaches into the core of the
human person not only as a physical being but also as a spiritual being.
This "something," we believe, is God.❁

NOTES

[1] Almost all life on Earth as we know it depends on the sun, but there are strange forms of life, chemoheterotrophs, that live in geysers and deep sea channels, that do not draw their energy from the sun.

[2] Two primary texts served as references for this chapter: Cecie Starr and Ralph Taggart, *Biology: The Unity and Diversity of Life,* 7th ed. (Belmont, Calif.: Wadsworth, 1995) and Christopher Uhl, *Developing Ecological Consciousness: Pathways to a Sustainable World* (Lanham, Md.: Rowman and Littlefield, 2004). In an ecological context, nutrients are food elements essential for the nutrition of living organisms. A nutrient cycle is the movement from the organisms to their physical surroundings and back again, in a continuous cycle.

[3] David Suzuki and Amanda McConnell, *Sacred Balance: Rediscovering Our Place in Nature* (Vancouver, B.C.: Greystone, 1997).

[4] There also are algae and chlorophyll-like bacteria that also photosynthesize.

[5] Phytoplankton, or microscopic water-borne plants, are an important exception to this, and so are epiphytic plants, where most of the plant biodiversity in a rainforest is, and other unusual creatures like lichens.

[6] This image is from Uhl, p. 47.

[7] Uhl, *Developing Ecological Consciousness*, p. 82. Most people only know of *E. coli* through reports of food contamination. The vast majority of these bacteria are beneficial, but some are indeed harmful.

[8] Aldo Leopold, *A Sand County Almanac* (Oxford: Oxford University Press, 1949).

[9] Rachel Carson, *Silent Spring* (Boston: Houghton Mifflin, 1962).

[10] Theo Colborn, Dianne Dumanoski and John Peterson Myers, *Our Stolen Future: Are We Threatening Our Fertility, Intelligence, and Survival? A Scientific Detective Story* (New York: Dutton, 1996); Uhl, *Developing Ecological Consciousness*, pp. 210–219.

[11] World Commission on Economic Development, *Our Common Future* (Oxford: Oxford University Press, 1987).

[12] Mathis Wackernagel and William Rees, *Our Ecological Footprint: Reducing Human Impact on the Earth* (Philadelphia: New Society, 1996).

[chapter two]

IS CREATION THE HOUSE OF GOD?

The concept of *oikos* is an important one for understanding creation's web of life. It refers to the house where we humans physically live and the well-being of the house that makes it our home. By the end of reading the previously mentioned *At Home in the Cosmos* by David Toolan I could not help but ask, are we at home in the cosmos? Bonaventure captured the essential meaning of home when he wrote, "you exist more truly where you love than where you merely live."[1] Home is not simply the place to sleep or eat or to be physically sustained. Rather, to be at home is to experience freedom in love; where one loves there one is free and at home. If "home is where the heart is," then why is our home—the Earth—in peril? Do we love this home or simply use it? David Toolan's book reminds us that we may exist in a place, but if we do not love in that place then we truly do not live there. It is easy to disregard or destroy that which is unloved.

•

FRANCIS: AT HOME IN THE COSMOS

Francis of Assisi was at home in the cosmos. We know this because at the end of his life he composed the *Canticle of the Creatures* in which he sang of brotherhood and sisterhood in the family of creation: Brother Sun, Sister Moon, Sister Mother Earth. The cosmos became home to Francis because this is where he discovered love, the overflowing goodness of God. The brothers who lived with Francis remembered him as one who reverenced the Earth:

When he washed his hands, he chose a place where the water would not be trampled underfoot after the washing. Whenever he had to walk over rocks, he would walk with fear and reverence out of love for Him who is called "The Rock."...

He also told the brother who cut the wood for fire not to cut down the whole tree, but to cut in such a way that one part remained while another was cut....

He used to tell the brother who took care of the garden not to cultivate all the ground in the garden for vegetables, but to leave a piece of ground that would produce wild plants that in their season would produce "Brother Flowers." Moreover, he used to tell the brother gardener that he should make a beautiful flower bed in some part of the garden, planting and cultivating every variety of fragrant plants and those producing beautiful flowers.[2]

Francis taught the brothers to accept the gifts of God's goodness in creation and to respond with grateful hearts through bonds of love, care, concern and companionship. Francis valued the home of the earth not as *his* home alone but first and foremost as *God's* home.

•

CREATION V. NATURE

To speak of creation as our home is to speak of creation as relationship. The word *creation* implies relationship, unlike the word *nature,* which holds no inherent religious meaning. "Creation" points to a "Creator," a God who creates. The distinction between creation and nature is an important one because when we discuss the integrity of nature, especially from the Franciscan tradition, we are really talking about creation, the relationship of the natural world, including humans, to the Creator. "Creation," therefore, means relationships between the human and non-human created order, the place of the human person within that order, and the response of the person to the created order in its relationship to God. In this respect, talk of an "environmental crisis" from a Franciscan perspective must immediately signal a "religious crisis" simply because environment is more than nature alone; rather, it is that realm of God's goodness in the natural world that shares with us humans a deep longing for God.

•

FRANCIS: THE FIRST ECOLOGIST

Francis of Assisi is an example of a religious person in the Christian tradition who stood rightly in creation. Francis was probably one of the first deep ecologists in the tradition without ever trying to be one.[3] Deep ecology was a movement that arose in the 1970s in response to the environmental crisis. It highlighted the fact that we humans stand *in* the web of life and not above or beyond it. The birth of Francis' "ecological self" began in the beautiful province of Umbria, with its breathtaking panorama of valleys and mountains. He was born into a merchant class family and received a basic education in reading and writing in the local church school of Assisi. Since he had not been trained as an intellectual in his youth, he never absorbed the Christian Neoplatonic attitude toward creation that occupied the discussions of students at the University of Paris. Neoplatonism was a hierarchical way of viewing God and the world and passed into the Middle Ages through the writings of Augustine and Pseudo-Dionysius, among others. The Neoplatonic ladder of ascent presented a movement away from, and rising above natural, sensible things as if they were inferior and, in some sense, not truly real.[4] The emphasis on spirit over matter according to a hierarchy of being meant an intellectualizing of mystical experience.[5] The Neoplatonists, therefore, turned quickly from the material world and its individual creatures to scale the metaphysical ladder to the spiritual and divine realms by means of universal concepts.[6]

Francis came from a base of popular and lay experience. His family was part of the rising merchant class in Assisi. His father was a cloth merchant and owned a shop in Assisi where Francis worked for some time. Francis was not only familiar with the daily business of buying and trading cloth but he came into contact with many different types of people—farmers, craftsmen, artists, bakers—people who worked with their hands and valued the material things of the earth. The idea of transcending this world to contemplate true reality, like the Neoplatonists, would have been foreign to Francis' thinking. Rather, he regarded earthly life as possessing ideal, positive potential as God's creation. Zachary Hayes writes, "[Francis] was profoundly in love with the world of material reality. Indeed, his was a spirituality that did not turn him away from the physical world, but led him to embrace it in a new way."[7] Some regard him as "the first materialist" in the best sense of the word because of the way he looked on the material world—not for *what* it is but for *how* it is—God's creation.[8]

The town of Assisi where Francis grew up was influenced by the Cathar heresy, a belief in a dualistic system that taught that matter was created by an evil god and spirit by a good god. Cathars held that there are two creators: one of invisible things, whom they called the benevolent god (or "good" god), and another of visible things, whom they named the malevolent god (or "evil" god). They attributed the New Testament to the good god, but the Old Testament to the evil god, rejecting it altogether, except certain authorities that are inserted in the New Testament from the Old Testament, which they esteemed worthy of reception.[9] The Cathar heresy was immensely popular, especially throughout northern and central Italy and southern France. The popularity of this belief probably lay in the fact that medieval Europe experienced profound suffering on many different levels. In the area of Assisi, for example, lack of work, exploitation by those who assigned work, illness due to lack of hygiene, wars and famine were common among the people, especially those of lower rank. Through the theology of the Cathars, one could explain the suffering of this world as the result of an evil god. Catharism offered a path to salvation by escaping the evil of matter and entering into the realm of light through knowledge of the Gospels.[10] Hence, it advocated a type of Gnosticism or salvation through knowledge alone. Its interpretation of the Gospel led to a rejection of the world and the suffering within it.

Although some might see a dualism in Francis of Assisi who spoke of "hatred of the body," such a view would be erroneous, for Francis saw material reality, including the body, as good. In his Fifth Admonition, for example, he said: "Consider, O human being, in what great excellence the Lord God has placed you, for He created and formed you *to the image* of his beloved Son according to the body and *to His likeness* according to the Spirit."[11] This is hardly the insight of one who thinks matter is evil. His disdain for the body focused on attitudes or behaviors that led to broken relationships and prevented the goodness of the body from shining out. We might assume, however, that his liberal youth influenced his view of the body as well. His first biographer, Thomas of Celano, tells us that as a young man, Francis was a libertine, a spendthrift and rather vain. He loved fine parties, foolish talk and the esteem of others. The young Francis probably had little care or concern for the world of nature, as the center of his attention seemed to be himself. The direction of his life began to change, however, when Francis' desire for the glory of knighthood was thwarted. He was wounded in battle and while convalescing in a soldiers' hospital, he began to ponder the meaning of his life. This period marked the beginning of Francis' conversion. Thomas of Celano writes that around this time, "the beauty of the fields, the delight of the vineyards, and whatever else was beautiful to see could offer him no delight at all."[12] The search for meaning and purpose in his life led Francis to withdraw from his circle of friends and to search out abandoned places in order to pray. One day he wandered into the dilapidated church of San Damiano on the outskirts of Assisi. Upon entering the church he saw a large Byzantine cross of the crucified and risen Christ. While praying before the cross, he heard the words, "Francis, go rebuild My house; as you see, it is all being destroyed."[13] "From that time on," Thomas writes, "compassion for the Crucified was impressed into his holy soul."[14] In this early stage of his conversion, we might say that Francis was "grasped" by the overwhelming love of God, a love that "seized" him in the core of his being. According to Bonaventure's account, Francis' *"soul melted* at the sight, and the memory of Christ's passion was so impressed on the innermost recesses of his heart."[15] This "heart-centered" encounter with the crucified Christ, as Bonaventure describes it, suggests that what took place in Francis touched the core of his personhood. His experience of God's overflowing love turned him in a new direction. The search for meaning, purpose and openness to God—as the love of God penetrated his soul—changed Francis' life forever and marked the beginning of his impact on history.

The life of Francis shows us that right relationship in creation is not easy. He heard the words spoken by the crucified Christ, "go rebuild my house" and took them literally. He began to rebuild the church of San Damiano stone by stone. But as he reflected on these words, he came to understand a deeper meaning of them in his life. His devotion to Mary, the mother of God, led him to realize that the "house of God" is, first, the human person. The Word dwells in human flesh not in stone buildings. As the Word dwells in the human person, so too the same Word dwells in creation. The Word who is made flesh in the person of Jesus Christ is the same Word through whom all things are made. Fish, water, trees, birds, air, wind, fire—all are created through the Word of God. What Francis heard originally, "go, rebuild my house" became much larger for him; it became the entire *oikos.* "Go, rebuild my *oikos;* as you see, it is all being destroyed." The Incarnation of God opened up the eyes of Francis to the inner truth of creation as the very place where God is revealed—or concealed when humans fail to see God humbly present in the magnificent diversity of creation.

•

BONAVENTURE: THE KEY TO UNDERSTANDING

CREATION AND INCARNATION

Francis' understanding of God influenced the theologian Bonaventure.[16] It is Bonaventure who helps us understand more clearly the integral relationship between creation and Incarnation through his theology of the Trinity. This relationship is important to understand because when we talk about solar energy, complex sugars, insects and plant-eating animals, we are ultimately talking about God. Life's essentials do not simply "appear;" they have an origin. Unless we know their origin, we cannot know the destiny of all that is life-giving in creation. Bonaventure believed that a God who could create is one who could communicate divine life to others. Only a self-communicative God, he said, could be a creator God. And if communication marks God's life, then God must be a plurality of persons, a Trinity. Bonaventure drew from two other theologians, Pseudo-Dionysius and Richard of St. Victor, to understand the Trinity. Pseudo-Dionysius described the Trinity as self-diffusive goodness while Richard said it was marked by a communion of persons in love. The life of the Trinity originates eternally from the first divine Person, the Father who is infinitely fecund and thus a fountain full of goodness. This Fountain Fullness expresses itself perfectly in the one who is Son and Word. This process reaches its consummation in the love between them, which is the Spirit. Love, according to Bonaventure, is the energizing spirit of the dynamic life of the Trinity. The second and third Persons of the Trinity flow from a generosity of love and of willing, originating in the One who is boundless and inexhaustible love.[17]

The key to Bonaventure's theology of creation lies in the Trinity, in the eternal generation of the Word from the Father. The Father, who is without beginning, is totally self-communicative and communicates the entirety of his ideas to another. The self-communicative goodness of the Father is literally God giving Godself away—but in such a way that fecundity marks the Trinity's dynamic, eternal life. This total expression of the Father is the Word, who proceeds from the Father as the Father's perfect self-expression and Image. The Word is the exemplar or model for all that exists. As the full and total expression of God's primal fruitfulness, the Son is also the expression of all that God can be in relation to the finite.[18] Thus, the relation between the Father and Son is the first and primal relation and the basis for all other relations.

Bonaventure saw that just as the Word is the inner self-expression of God, the created order is the external expression of the inner Word. Creation flows out of the love between the Father and Son. It is a limited expression of the infinite and dynamic love between the Father and Son united in the Spirit. Creation is an external "word" of God. This finite "word" of God is the one eternal Word expressed in time and history. Creation, therefore, is the "speech" of God. That is why it is referred to as a "book." God speaks Godself in the diverse variety of creation.[19] In this respect, creation is not a mere external act of God, an object on the fringe of divine power; rather, it is rooted in the self-diffusive goodness of God's inner life and emerges out of the innermost depths of Trinitarian life. The possibility of God's creative activity rests in his being Triune, which is to say that God could not communicate being to the finite if God were not supremely communicative in himself.[20] To say that creation shares in the mystery of the Trinity means that it is caught up in the dynamic process of self-transcendence and self-communication of interpenetrating relationships and creative love. Creation expresses who God is as love in such a way that God who is Trinity loves the world with the very same love with which God eternally is.

Bonaventure described the created universe as the Fountain Fullness of God's expressed being. As God expresses himself in creation, creation, in turn, expresses the Creator. We can compare the manifold variety of things in creation to the stained-glass windows of a great cathedral. Just as light strikes the various panes of glass and diffracts into an array of colors, so too the divine light emanates through the Word and diffracts in the universe, producing a myriad of "colors" expressed in a myriad of things, all reflecting the divine light in some way. Bonaventure used two images to describe creation: mirror and book—two images that connote relationship. Let us take a look first at the image of the mirror. All of creation—rocks, trees, stars, plants, animals and humans—in some way reflects the power, wisdom and goodness of the Trinity. God shines through creation and the face of God is reflected in creation precisely by the way things express themselves.[21] Creation therefore is a mirror of God. The created world, however, is also a book in which its Maker, the Trinity, shines forth and is represented at three levels of expression: a trace (vestige), an image, and a likeness.[22] In his small "handbook of theology" the *Breviloquium*, Bonaventure wrote:

> From all we have said, we may gather that the created world is a kind of book reflecting, representing, and describing its Maker, the Trinity, at three different levels of expression: as a vestige, as an image, and as a likeness. The aspect of vestige ("footprint") is found in every creature; the aspect of image, only in intelligent creatures or rational spirits; the aspect of likeness, only in those spirits that are God-conformed. Through these successive levels, comparable to steps, the human intellect is designed to ascend gradually to the supreme Principle, which is God.[23]

In every creature, therefore, the first Person of the Trinity is reflected as the power that holds the creature in being. The second Person is reflected as the Wisdom or the Exemplar, by which it is created. The third Person is reflected as the goodness that will bring the creature to its consummation.[24] The difference in these levels of expression reflects the degree of similarity between the creature and Creator. The trace (or vestige) is the most distant reflection of God and is found in all creatures. That is, every grain of sand, every star, every earthworm, reflects the Trinity as its origin, its reason of existence and the end to which it is destined. The image, however, is only found in intellectual (human) beings. It reflects the fact that the human person is not only created according to the image of the Trinity, but as image, the human person is capable of union with the divine. Bonaventure says that those humans conformed to God by grace bear a likeness to God. Thus in Bonaventure's view, every creature is understood as an aspect of God's self-expression in the world, and since every creature has its foundation in the Word, each is equally close to God (although the mode of relationship differs). God is profoundly present to all things and God is expressed in all things, so that each creature is a symbol and a sacrament of God's presence and Trinitarian life.[25] The world is created as a means of God's self-revelation so that, like a mirror or footprint, it might lead us to love and praise the Creator. We are created to read the book of creation so that we may know the "Author of Life." This book of creation is an expression of who God is and is meant to lead humans to what it signifies, namely, the eternal Trinity of dynamic, self-diffusive love.

The profound reflection of God throughout creation signifies that the created world is a sacrament of God. "The term 'sacrament,'" David Toolan writes, "derived from the Roman soldier's solemn promise to serve the emperor. When Christians adopted the word for their rites of initiation and blessing, it came to mean the human act of giving a sensible sign...that confers God's promise and grace."[26] Bonaventure's sacramental vision of creation not only speaks of God's promise and grace, but creation expresses who God is; it is God's mirror and book. God's glory is reflected in the sacred order of creation. Because the world expresses the Word through whom all things are made (John 1:1), every creature is in itself a "little word" of God. In this respect, the whole creation is both sacramental and incarnational, that is, every aspect of creation is a "little Incarnation" of the divine Word. That is why when Jesus came there was a perfect fit between God and creation.

•

JOHN DUNS SCOTUS AND THE GOODNESS OF CREATION

While Bonaventure described an intimate link between the Trinity and creation, the fourteenth-century philosopher and theologian John Duns Scotus viewed the goodness of creation in three ways: as the primacy of Christ, the freedom of God and the contingency of the world.[27] Scotus looked at our world and realized that God is absolutely free, nothing created is necessary. Since God did not have to create anything, all is gift and grace.[28] God creates because God wishes to reveal and communicate himself to others as the fullness of God's own love. God chose to create this world precisely as it is to reveal divine love. The present moment, therefore, expresses the perfection of the eternal. God creates, Scotus claims, for God's own purpose, namely, the glory and love of God. Creation is simply the work of an infinitely loving Creator. Scotus, like Francis and Bonaventure, saw an intimate connection between creation and Incarnation, a connection that he grounded in the infinite love of God. The reason for all divine activity, he said, is found in the very nature of God as love. God is Trinity and Trinity means three divine Persons in a communion of love. As the eternal movement of lover (Father), beloved (Son) and the sharing of love (Spirit), the Trinity is the model of reality, especially for human relationships.

According to Scotus, God's love is ordered, free and holy. Every single aspect of the created universe exists because of God's absolute freedom and because of God's unlimited love. All of creation is a gift. Nothing in creation is necessary.[29] God also loves himself in others and this love is unselfish since God is the cause of all creatures. This divine love tends to "spill over" or diffuse itself, and God wills that God be loved by another who can love him as perfectly as God loves himself. This "other" of God's infinite love is Jesus Christ. Scotus believed that God became human in Jesus out of love (rather than sin) because God wanted to express himself outwardly in a creature who would be a masterpiece and love God perfectly in return. Christ, therefore, is the first in God's intention to love and thus to create. Creation is not an independent act of divine love that was, incidentally, followed up by divine self-revelation in the covenant. Rather, the divine desire to become incarnate was part of the overall plan or order of intention. Scotus places the Incarnation within the context of creation and not human sin. Christ is the masterpiece of love, the greatest work of God. The idea that all of creation is made for Christ means that for Christ to come about there had to be a creation, and then the creation of beings capable of understanding and freely responding to divine initiative. Creation was only a prelude to a much fuller manifestation of divine goodness, namely, the

Incarnation.[30] Christ is the meaning and model of creation and every creature is made in the image of Christ. Because creation is centered on the Incarnation, every leaf, cloud, fruit, animal and person is an outward expression of the Word of God in love. When Jesus comes as the Incarnation of God, there is a "perfect fit" because everything has been made to resemble Jesus Christ.[31] This means that sun, moon, trees, animals, stories all have life only in Christ, through Christ and with Christ, for Christ is the Word through whom all things are made (cf. John 1:1).[32]

For Scotus, Christ is the blueprint for creation. As the motif or pattern of creation, Christ is the perfect divine-human communion who exemplifies the meaning and purpose of all creation, namely, the praise and glory of God in a communion of love. All of creation is to be transformed into a communion of love centered in Christ. Scotus's theology of creation is one in which grace and nature intertwine. Nothing in creation is accidental or excessive; nothing is worthless or trivial. Each and every thing, no matter how small or seemingly insignificant, is of infinite value because it reflects God in its own unique being. Because God's being is the foundation of the natural order, the ineffable is made tangible through the concrete existence of all reality. For Scotus, God's being shines from within created being. Creation is like a lamp in which each unique created being radiates the light of God. What we humans are called to do is to observe closely, attentively and carefully that things are what they are and do what they do. And it is in being themselves that they are Christ—words of God incarnate.[33] To really know Christ, therefore, we must live attentively to the particularities of creation. Without such attention we can easily lose living contact with Christ in his most widely extended body, the universe.

The relation between creation and Incarnation speaks to us of a God who is in relation to us and desires to share life with us. The God who brings all things into being through love desires to bring to perfection all that exists in love. Christ is the center of that love. Incarnation is key to understanding creation, and creation is essential for the

Incarnation. God's dream for creation is made known in Jesus Christ. Francis of Assisi was not a trained theologian, but he did have insight into the Incarnation, as it spoke to him of God's personal love for creation. When we view the relationship between Incarnation and creation in the life of Francis, we see an ordering of love: first, a grasp of God's love in his own life; second, a realization that he was loved by God and thus called to love himself; third, a love of the human person outside himself signified by the leper, followed by a love of creatures. To put this progression of love in another way, once Francis experienced the love of God in his own life, he could begin to experience that love in other persons, in all creatures large and small and in the diverse things of creation. Love forged Francis into an "ecological brother."

•

WHO AM I? IDENTITY AND THE CREATED SELF

The key to Francis' fraternal relationship to the created world is identity. Francis came to know himself as a creature in relation to God as Creator. "The secret of my full identity is hidden in Him," Thomas Merton wrote.[34] When I find God, then I find myself, and when I find myself then I find the person I am created to be, the little "word" that God has spoken from all eternity. Bonaventure, too, wrote: "I see myself better in God than in myself."[35] Only when we know the source of our lives can we know the truth of our lives—that we and all creation come from God and belong to God. We are not created to wield power over others but to join with others, including the created world, in the praise of God. Without this discovery of true identity, we go about in the world with a false sense of self, a self far away from God and from the true self. We begin to wander in the world looking for the meaning of our lives, which leads to self-centeredness and a detachment from the created world around us. The false self thrives on power and manipulation because it does not know the true self and therefore does not know itself in God. The false self is not at home in the *oikos* because it is not at home with itself.

In his *Major Legend of Saint Francis* Bonaventure described Francis as one who lived in the center of creation because he lived in relation to Christ the center. In and through his relationship with Christ, Francis discovered that God is love and love requires relationship with another. In the early phase of his conversion, following his encounter with the crucified Christ at San Damiano, Francis was led to the lepers, the poor and the sick. Through reflection on his life we realize that to love the fragile and weak things of nature, we must first love the fragile and weak human person—the poor and sick—the lepers among us. The encounter with Christ crucified helped him understand that God humbly bends low in love and hides in weak and fragile forms. Every person and creature is uniquely loved by God. Although Francis had a disdain for lepers in his youth, his experience of God's love in Christ changed him. After he felt the kiss of God in his own life, he desired to kiss the lepers, give them his clothes and to be with them. He tells us that in kissing the leper, what was bitter became sweet.[36] Francis' radical need to be close to the sick and the lepers flowed from his *I-Thou* experience of God and his understanding of Christ as poor and humble. When he realized that Incarnation means "God with us"—God dwelling in fragile, human flesh—he discovered the all-powerful goodness of God hidden in the disfigured flesh of the leper, in the sick and the poor, in earthworms and tiny creatures. Francis discovered that he could not be an "I" without a "Thou," and that relationship is essential to personhood.

Bonaventure viewed the life of Francis as one of growth in awareness of divine goodness at the heart of the world in and through the mystery of Christ.[37] "In beautiful things," Bonaventure wrote, "he saw Beauty itself and through his vestiges imprinted on creation he followed his Beloved everywhere…he savored in each and every creature that Goodness which is their fountain source."[38] Through prayer, poverty and attentiveness to the detail of the other, Francis discovered a God of humble love expressed in ordinary, fragile human flesh and in the simple things of creation. He would call creatures, no matter how small, by the name of "brother" or "sister," Bonaventure claimed, "because he knew they shared with him the same beginning."[39] Thomas of Celano wrote that

> Even for worms he had a warm love, since he had read this text about the Savior: *I am a worm and not a man*. That is why he used to pick them up from the road and put them in a safe place so that they would not be crushed by the footsteps of passersby....
>
> Whenever he found an abundance of flowers, he used to preach to them and invite them to praise the Lord, just as if they were endowed with reason.[40]

Rather than viewing the world from the top rung of the ladder of creation, Francis saw himself as part of creation. His was a descending solidarity between humanity and creation. Instead of using creatures to ascend to God, he found God in all creatures and identified with them as brother and sister because he recognized that he shared with them the same primordial source of goodness.

In light of Francis, we are called to participate in life-giving relationships that reflect a God of generous love. Sin describes the personal history of one who was created for communion and refuses it.[41] It is the rejection of our identity as part of an interdependent world in which God's power as creative source expresses itself through the shared power of other creatures.[42] Sin is the refusal to accept responsibility for those to whom we are connected; thus, it is the refusal to accept the "other" of the relationship (the "Thou") as the one who addresses us, discloses our responsibility and calls us into question.[43] The wages of sin are exile and loneliness in the land of unrelatedness. Because sin is the failure to accept the other, the Thou, as part of who I am, sin reveals its face in radical individualism, a deadness of personhood manifested in an "I-It" relation. In an "I-It" relation, Richard Gaillardetz states, we objectify the world around us, placing everything into distinct categories and imposing order on our world. In the I-Thou relation, we do not seek to objectify the world, making it accessible for manipulation and control by putting people and things into their respective categories; rather, we move out to the world in a stance of attentiveness, becoming present, vulnerable and receptive to what the world has to offer.[44]

Francis moved out into the world in attentiveness and openness. He encountered a living God in creation—a "Thou"—which gave him insight to the goodness of creatures, despite their limitations and sometimes brokenness. Scotus used the term *haecceitas* or "thisness" to describe the unique dignity not only of human persons but of all created reality. Each created being, whether it is a human person, a tree or a bee, has a distinct "thisness" that distinguishes it from other similar creatures. *Haecceitas* refers to that which is intrinsic, unique and proper to Being itself; that which makes a singular "this" and "not-that" and which sets it off from other things like it (or of the same nature). It can only be known by direct acquaintance, not from any consideration of more general categories. We might say it signifies that deeper reality within each being that is knowable to God alone—the sacredness of each being—which cannot be duplicated or cloned.[45]

Jim Edmiston describes how his insight to the world of biodiversity changed after he began to study the world of the *Nostima* fly larva. He writes: "After I saw the world from the perspective of a fly larva, the world never looked the same. Each living creature becomes an instrument of creation that cries out to be respected for its role and for its individuality."[46] By entering into the universe of the fly larva, Edmiston realized that the smallest environmental disturbances can affect individual living creatures. "We don't need to save species," he claims "we need to build relationships with other species."[47] How do we begin to build relationships with the myriad of types of species surrounding us, unless we begin to have some contact with them and acknowledge their "thisness"?

Scotus's notion of *haecceitas* suggests that attentiveness to the details of created reality is necessary if we are to live within the constraints of a finite creation. Attentiveness means relating to that which exists not as object or idol but as icon through which the infinite goodness of God radiates—like Edmiston—realizing that even a fly bears a unique goodness. When we lose sight of the uniqueness of created being then things become "its," objects of manipulation and control, only to be given value or life by the one who controls or manipulates it. When things lose their intrinsic goodness and become lifeless objects, they lose their distinct place in nature or creation. The *oikos* becomes disrupted, species are destroyed, and biodiverse nature is extinguished for a shopping mall or condominiums. Creation is unraveled.

•

IDENTITY IN GOD

The life of Francis shows us that to appreciate the book of creation we must come to know ourselves as creatures of God and as creatures of creation. Without self-knowledge there can be no real knowledge of creation as our home and the womb of our birth. Without the human person to give voice to creation, to celebrate its giftedness and sacredness, creation becomes mute and vulnerable to manipulation. The key to creation's holiness, therefore, is in human identity—who we are in our Creator, the Trinity of divine love. This identity is revealed to us in Jesus Christ, the Word in whom we are made flesh. If God is alive in us, as he was in Francis, then we are alive to the world of God's good creation. However, if God is dead in us, then we are dead to the deeper meaning of creation as well. Francis realized that God humbly bends low in love and hides in simple, ordinary, fragile beings. So too we must realize that God is in our midst. Only when we can recognize creatures for what they are—expressions of God's overflowing love—can we recognize the source of our own lives as well. The love that gave birth to all creatures is the same love that has brought us into existence. This is what Francis realized, the luminous web of God's love revealed in Jesus Christ. We are called to live in this luminous web of love.

NOTES

[1] Bonaventure, *Soliloquium*, 2.12 (VIII, 49), vol. 2. Zachary Hayes, trans. *Bonaventure: Mystical Writings* (New York: Crossroad, 1999), p. 140.

[2] "The Assisi Compilation," 88, in *FA:ED*, vol. 2, p. 192.

[3] Keith Warner, O.F.M., "Was St. Francis a Deep Ecologist?" In Albert LaChance and John E. Carroll, eds. *Embracing Earth: Catholic Approaches to Ecology* (Maryknoll, N.Y.: Orbis, 1994), pp. 225–240.

[4] Sean Edward Kinsella, "How Great a Gladness: Some Thoughts on Francis of Assisi and the Natural World" *Studies in Spirituality*, vol. 12 (2002), p. 66. According to Plato's Allegory of the Cave, which was very influential on the structure of Neoplatonism, sensible reality is comprised of *ersatz* (artificial/substituted) forms while the true forms lie in a transcendent, spiritual world.

[5] Kinsella, 90; Ewert Cousins, "Francis of Assisi: Christian Mysticism at the Crossroads," in *Mysticism and Religious Traditions*, S. Katz, ed. (New York: Oxford, 1983), pp. 164–165.

[6] Roger D. Sorrell, *St. Francis of Assisi and Nature: Tradition and Innovation in Western Christian Attitudes toward the Environment* (New York: Oxford University Press, 1988), p. 89.

[7] Zachary Hayes, "Toward a Philosophy of Education in the Spirit of St. Bonaventure," in *Proceedings of the Seventh Centenary Celebration of the Death of Saint Bonaventure*, Pascal F. Foley, ed. (St. Bonaventure, N.Y.: Franciscan Institute, 1975), p. 18.

[8] Paul M. Allen and Joan deRis Allen, *Francis of Assisi's Canticle of the Creatures: A Modern Spiritual Path* (New York: Continuum, 1996), p. 45.

[9] Edward Peters, ed. *Heresy and Authority in Medieval Europe* (Philadelphia: University of Pennsylvania Press, 1980), p. 123.

[10] Raoul Manselli, *St. Francis of Assisi*, Paul Duggan, ed. (Chicago: Franciscan Herald, 1988), p. 5.

[11] Francis of Assisi, "Admonition V," in *FA:ED*, vol. 1, p. 131.

[12] Thomas of Celano, "The Life of Saint Francis," 2.3, in *FA:ED*, vol. 1, p. 185.

[13] Thomas of Celano, "The Remembrance of the Desire of a Soul," 6.10, in *FA:ED*, vol. 2, p. 249.

[14] Thomas of Celano, "The Remembrance of the Desire of a Soul," 6.10, in *FA:ED*, vol. 2, p. 249.

[15] Bonaventure, "The Major Legend of Saint Francis," 1.5 in *FA:ED*, vol. 2, p. 534.

[16] For a succinct read of Bonaventure's life and thought, see Ilia Delio, *Simply Bonaventure: An Introduction to His Life, Thoughts and Writings* (New York: New City, 2001).

[17] Janet C. Kwamme, "The *Fontalis Plenitudo* in Bonaventure as a Symbol for His Metaphysics," (unpublished PH.D. dissertation, Fordham University, 1999), p. 175.

[18] Zachary Hayes, introduction to *Disputed Questions on the Mystery of the Trinity*, vol. 3, *Works of Saint Bonaventure*, George Marcil, ed. (New York: Franciscan Institute, 1979), p. 47.

[19] In his *Commentary on Wisdom*, 13.5, Bonaventure says that "the entire world is, as it were, a kind of book in which the Creator can be known in terms of power, wisdom and goodness which shine through in creatures." Cited in Zachary Hayes, trans., *Bonaventure: Mystical Writings* (New York: Crossroad, 1999), p. 64.

[20] Zachary Hayes, "Christology and Metaphysics in the Thought of Bonaventure," *Journal of Religion* (Supplement, 1978), p. 91.

[21] Bonaventure, *Itinerarium Mentis in Deum* 2.1 (V, 300).

[22] Bonaventure, *Breviloquium* 2.12 (V, 230), p. 96.

[23] Bonaventure, *Breviloquium* 2.12 (V, 230), p. 96.

[24] Denis Edwards, "The Discovery of Chaos and the Retrieval of the Trinity," in *Chaos and Complexity: Scientific Perspectives on Divine Action* (Rome: Vatican Observatory Publications, 1995), p. 162.

[25] Edwards, p. 163.

[26] David Toolan, *At Home in the Cosmos* (Maryknoll, N.Y.: Orbis, 2003), pp. 33–34.

[27] For an introduction to the life and thought of John Duns Scotus see Richard Cross, *Duns Scotus* (New York: Oxford, 1999); Mary Beth Ingham, *Scotus for Dunces: A Simple Guide to the Subtle Doctor* (New York: Franciscan Institute, 2003).

[28] Kenan B. Osborne, "Incarnation, Individuality and Diversity," *The Cord* 45.3 (1995): 22; John Duns Scotus, *A Treatise on God as First Principle*, Allan B. Wolter, trans. (Chicago: Franciscan Herald, 1966), p. xvii.

[29] Osborne, p. 70.

[30] Ingham, pp. 56–57.

[31] Ingham, p. 264.

[32] Ingham, p. 266.

[33] William Short, "Pied Beauty: Gerard Manley Hopkins and the Scotistic View of Nature," *The Cord* 45.3 (1995), p. 32.

[34] Thomas Merton, *New Seeds of Contemplation* (New York: New Directions, 1961), p. 33.

[35] Bonaventure, Hex. 12.9 (V, 385) De Vinck, "On Six Days of Creation," p. 177.

[36] Francis of Assisi, "Testament," 3, in *FA:ED*, vol. 1, p. 124.

[37] See Ilia Delio, "Identity and Difference in Bonaventure's *Legenda maior*," *Studies in Spirituality* 13 (2003), pp. 199–211.

[38] Bonaventure, *Legenda maior*, 9.1., Ewert Cousins, trans. in *Bonaventure: The Soul's Journey into God, The Tree of Life, The Major Life of St. Francis* (Mahwah, N.J.: Paulist, 1978), p. 263.

[39] Bonaventure, *Legenda maior*, 8.6., Cousins, trans. pp. 254–255.

[40] Thomas of Celano, "The Life of Saint Francis," in *FA:ED*, vol. 1, pp. 250–251.

[41] Jane Kopas, *Sacred Identity, Sacred Identity: Exploring a theology of the person* (Mahwah, N.J.: Paulist, 1994), p. 103.

[42] Kopas, p. 103.

[43] Adriaan Theodoor Peperzak, *Beyond: The Philosophy of Emmanuel Levinas* (Evanston, Ill: Northwestern University Press, 1997), p. 175; Robyn Horner, *Rethinking God as Gift: Marion, Derrida and the Limits of Phenomenology* (New York: Fordham, 2001), pp. 64–66.

[44] Richard R. Gaillardetz, *Transforming Our Days: Spirituality, Community and Liturgy in a Technological Culture* (New York: Crossroad, 2000), p. 57.

[45] See Ingham, pp. 53–54.

[46] James F. Edmiston, "How to Love a Worm," in *Franciscan Theology of the Environment*, p. 388.

[47] Edmiston, p. 388.

chapter three

EMBODYING THE INCARNATE WORD IN CREATION

Francis' relationship to the created world captures our imagination. As we read in the last chapter, "once Francis experienced the love of God in his own life, he could begin to experience that love in other persons and in tiny creatures." His worldview differed vastly from our contemporary view of seeing ourselves as separate from creation. In modern-day terms Francis lived out of his *ecological self*, a wider, interconnected sense of self that is rooted in the fact of our interconnectedness with all of life. His identity did not stop at his "skin-enclosed self"[1] (man, brother, son, merchant, Italian) but extended out to include his membership in the created order, his status as one of the Creator's creatures.

Francis teaches us that God is incarnate in all of creation, and that entering into the cloister of creation helps us to deepen our relationship with our Creator. We have been given powerful gifts to explore this kinship: gifts we sometimes do not associate with our spiritual life or think of as potential tools with which to discover the Incarnation. God has generously bestowed us with amazing sensory abilities—thus we are fine-tuned to read the Book of Creation. Guided meditations that use our senses can teach us to read the "first book of revelation" anew. In addition, knowledge and understanding from science can aid us in understanding our place in the majesty of the created world, and this can greatly enhance our prayer life.

This chapter nurtures a Franciscan approach to the ecological self through reflection and spiritual practice, thus cultivating greater empathy toward all of creation. The guided meditation invites us to contemplate God's presence incarnate in the basic elements of our planet, helping us to *live into* the experience of being part of—rather than separate and distinct from—the Incarnation. Using our God-given abilities to know and to sense can help us to pay close attention to the created world, allowing us to encounter Christ. With Francis, our sense of self inevitably expands out to include Brother Sun, Sister Moon, Brother Air and our Sister Mother Earth, as we contemplate the gifts they give to us daily. Reflection questions and reflective actions that follow allow individuals or groups to further explore the ecological self and the implications it might have for our relationship with the larger world.

Before you begin to practice the following reflexive actions, please refer to the "Using the Method of Reflexive Action" suggestions in Appendix A. Once you have familiarized yourself with the format as presented, feel free to modify the prayer by adding different people or creatures to make the prayer more individually suited to your experience.

• •

GUIDED MEDITATION:
COMING HOME TO THE
INCARNATION IN CREATION

As you begin your sacred time, find a comfortable position and close your eyes. Bring your attention to your breath and allow your body to relax. Scan your body, your heart and your mind. Without judgment, notice where you are today. Letting go of any activities you have done or things yet to do, just settle into this present moment. Watch as thoughts come and go. As they arise, imagine them as a leaf or a feather, letting go as they float gently on the breeze to settle onto the earth. (Pause.)

Now notice the weight of your body against your chair or the ground. Some parts of your body rest more heavily against the chair or the ground than others. Imagine each of these points of contact relaxing a little and melting toward the earth. (Pause.) Feel the solidity of the earth and the way it holds you. Relax into this, letting gravity help you turn your tension over to the earth. As the earth absorbs your tension, and your muscles relax, feel gravity working on you and holding you safely against the earth. God desires our closeness and connection with the earth, which holds us close like a mother through its gravitational pull. Every planet and star, every human and animal, every rock and tree and plant, every molecule and every atom are attracted to one another through this basic force that binds the universe together into one big cosmic family.[2] Now listen to your heart beating and relax even more into this solidity. (Pause.)

Saint Francis of Assisi loved the earth; he walked respectfully over the land as holy ground. When he walked over rocks, "he would walk with fear and reverence out of love for Him who is called 'the Rock.'" We too are called to tread lightly on our planet, always supported by our Earth home, which has been created to sustain us in every moment. (Pause.)

Now bring your attention to your breath. Simply notice your breath, with no need to change it in any way. When your mind wanders, gently nudge it back to the breath, letting it rest there. Let your mind stay passive yet alert as your body begins to relax. (Pause.) Bring to your awareness the fact that your breath happens by itself. Even when you are not mindful of it, the Spirit of Life breathes through you in every moment of your life. Spend some time now nurturing an awareness of this miracle of breath. (Pause.) Now bring to mind the air that extends out from your breath, moving beyond you to fill the whole sky, joining with the great winds that encircle our planet. From the oceans to the deserts to the wind over high alpine meadows, our home planet is refreshed by this life-giving air, which moves across its surface in currents of wind and weather. Our thin layer of atmosphere miraculously protects the fragility of life on this planet. (Pause.) With Francis, we can dance with Brother Wind, and gaze upon Sister Moon and the stars, contemplating the vastness of God revealed to us in our universe home. We can be mindful that this precious air connects us to one another, across the globe and through the ages. This same air we breathe was breathed by our ancestors, by saints and sinners throughout time, by Francis himself. It will continue to circulate in this way until our children and great-great-grandchildren also breathe it through their lungs, so that they too may be filled with life. (Pause.)

Now picture the sun wherever it is in the sky. Each morning our planet turns toward the sun, soaking in its warmth and suckling its life energy. In each second our great, generous sun offers up four million tons of itself, transformed into radiant light and energy daily, free for all of life on Earth to use.[3] Green plants have evolved to take in this energy from the sun and convert it to food and energy for themselves. By doing so, plants feed all life on this planet as they make that energy available to humans and other mammals to ingest when we eat. All life depends on energy, and all energy has the sun as its ultimate source. With Francis, we too revel in the miracle of Brother Sun, whose life-giving energy courses through our own bodies too: warming our hearts, igniting our dreams and fueling our work in the world. (Pause.)

Now bring to mind the element of water in our blue-green planet home; the great oceans that cover two-thirds of its surface, the streams and rivers and lakes. Picture, too, the huge glaciers and snow-capped mountains that hold our water in reserve for us, releasing it slowly over time for the use of all

living beings, and the ice caps that cool our poles and play such
a key role in the circulation of air and water throughout our
planet. Give thanks for the water cycle that draws all this water
into our atmosphere, circulating the water across the world,
bringing the cleansing rains that feed all of life. We take in this
water: It composes 70 percent of our bodies and is contained
in each and every cell and in our blood and our tears. (Pause.)
Those who lived with Francis tell of him reverencing water by
choosing to wash his hands "where the water would not be
trampled underfoot after washing." With Francis, we marvel at
the wonder of water and honor the lifeblood of our bodies and
our bounteous earth.

Like all living creatures, we humans need food, a home
and a family, and none other exists for us or any other living
creature than our planet Earth. Walking with Francis through
God's house, honoring each of the elements of creation, we are
awed by the amazing hospitality of our planet home. (Pause.)
We prodigal sons and daughters can learn to fall in love again
with our planet home, and come to more fully appreciate our
utter dependence on its bounty. We can follow Francis' example of remembering that the earth is not our home alone, but
is first and foremost God's house. We can build anew bonds of
love, care, concern and companionship with not only our
human brothers and sisters, but with the house of creation that
sustains us and is kin to us all. We can walk in God's
Incarnation daily, remembering that the face of the Divine
shines through each and every thing, no matter how small or
seemingly insignificant. Through creation, the ineffable is
made tangible, and we can sense the radiance of God in the
beauty of the natural order.

Now sit for a few moments in silence, letting yourself rest into the experience of this meditation with a grateful heart for all that our Creator has given us. (Pause.) Bring your attention back to your breath, resting it there for a few moments, and when you are ready, open your eyes.

•   •   •   •   •   •   •   •   •   •   •   •   •   •   •   •   •   •   •

REFLECTION QUESTIONS TO NURTURE OUR ECOLOGICAL SELF

The planet is withering because we've accepted a sense of ourselves that is too small.[4]

In large part, we live out of a societal worldview that is mechanistic and reductive. Our planetary home has been dismantled and reduced to a commodity, its worth defined by its usefulness and profitability to this dominant world faith, consumerism.[5] Our children are taught as early as age three to define themselves primarily as "consumer."[6] We suffer from a limited sense of identity within this reductive worldview, and as a result, we witness destruction of life today on a scale confronted by no previous generation in recorded history.

With our common understanding of a separate self comes the perception that the earth is "out there" and thus our human attempt to protect it is defined as an altruistic duty. However, if our sense of self becomes rooted in our kinship with creation, as Francis' was, we will naturally be moved to protect our home, because we must protect that which we love and to which we belong. For us contemporary Christians, moving from an "I-It" relationship with the created world to an "I-Thou" relationship can transform our way of being in the world. Francis models how to live in right relationship with the world. The following reflection questions and practices encourage us to examine the worldview out of which we in our society (often unconsciously) live and the implications of this worldview for our actions.

1. What are the implications of the dominant mechanistic worldview on your own identity? On the poor? On the Earth? On your relationship with God?

_____

_____

_____

_____

2. Our consumer-driven society actively encourages our identity as *consumer* rather than *child of God* or *kin with creation*. How hard is it to imagine yourself as participating in the metabolic dance of life rather than exclusively as a consumer?

_____

_____

_____

_____

3. Does your limited identity cause you to "wander aimlessly in the world looking for the meaning of life," as Francis did before his conversion? Do you think this distorted identity contributes to the modern-day ecological crises? If so, how?

_____

_____

_____

_____

4. How do you usually identify yourself? Are there times you forget your true identity and live out of a more narrow sense of self? Can you think of times when you have lived out of a sense of self that was more connected to God and the world as sacred? What factors contributed to each?

_____

_____

_____

_____

5. What is one shift you can make in your worldview to nurture a more Franciscan identity as a child of creation?

_____

_____

_____

_____

REFLECTIVE ACTIONS TO NURTURE OUR ECOLOGICAL SELF

1. Work the above *Coming Home to the Incarnation in Creation* meditation into your daily prayer for a week or a month and take one concept from it into your daily life. Notice if this changes your sense of identity in the world.

2. Count the blessings you receive from creation. Our consumerist culture breeds in us a constant state of dissatisfaction and a "not-enough" mentality, which in turn keeps us fueling the consumer machine and plundering our planet. The simple act of gratitude strengthens our appreciation of all that we have been given and makes us less susceptible to these cultural influences. In this way, Joanna Macy, a teacher in

deep ecology and systems theory, reminds us that "Gratitude is a culturally subversive act."[7]

3. Pray biblical passages that speak to the immanence of God in creation: Acts 17:28; Psalms 34 and 139; Isaiah 6:3; Job 38; Leviticus 25.[8] Write your favorites on note cards and take them with you to read when you are spending time in nature.

4. Pray with Francis and other creation mystics, like Teilhard de Chardin, Wendell Berry or Hildegard of Bingen, within our tradition who poetically speak to the Incarnation. This can ignite your imagination and fuel your sense of participation in creation.[9]

5. Integrate songs that praise creation into your personal prayer, group reflections, and into your grace before meals. The Franciscan musician Rufino Zaragoza has written beautiful music emphasizing many of the concepts in chapters one through three of this book, especially his song *Sacred Creation* (based on Francis' *Canticle of the Creatures*).[10]

6. Measure your ecological footprint. One good way to do this is to take the "Ecological Footprint Quiz" at the Redesigning Progress Web site which has an internal calculator to compute your results.[11] This is an excellent tool to identify some dimensions of the metabolic relationship between human society and the earth. Consider doing this with a friend, or with a group of friends, and compare your results. After doing so, spend some time reflecting on the implications of the size of your footprint, or refer to chapter twelve for more ideas of how to use this assessment tool.

• In regard to the footprint you leave in creation, what is required of you as a person of faith?

_____

_____

_____

_____

• List three ways that you (or your family) could begin to shrink your ecological footprint through reducing resources used in your home and lifestyle.

_____

_____

_____

_____

• List three ways that you (or your family) could begin to reduce the amount of waste that flows from your home and lifestyle.

_____

_____

_____

NOTES

[1] Joanna Macy, *Theory and Practice of the Work That Reconnects*, August, 2005.

[2] Brian Swimme, *The Universe Is a Green Dragon* (New Mexico: Bear, 1985), p. 49.

[3] Brian Swimme, *Hidden Heart of the Cosmos: Humanity and the New Story* (New York: Orbis, 1996), p. 39.

[4] Gail Worcelo, C.P., "Living at the Evolutionary Edge," workshop at the Northwest Catholic Women's Convocation, Seattle, Washington, April, 2005.

[5] Swimme, *Hidden Heart of the Cosmos,* pp. 13–20.

[6] Juliet Schor, *Born to Buy: The Commercialized Child and the New Consumer Culture* (New York: Scribner, 2004), p. 19.

[7] Joanna Macy, "Nature and the Sacred: A Fierce Green Fire" Conference, Oregon State University, October, 2004.

[8] Marcus Borg, "Nature and the Sacred: A Fierce Green Fire" Conference, Oregon State University, October, 2004.

[9] Some suggested reading of mystics include, but are not limited to: James W. Skehan, S.J., *Praying With Teilhard de Chardin: Companions for the Journey* (Winona, Minn.: St. Mary's, 2000) and Wendell Berry, *Sabbaths* (California: North Point, 1987).

[10] Rufino Zaragoza, *Love's Radiant Light* (Oregon: Oregon Catholic, 1991), p. 38.

[11] To calculate your ecological footprint, take the "Ecological Footprint Quiz" available at http://www.redefiningprogress.org or http://www.myfootprint.org.

[part two]

•

•

•

•

•

CREATION
AS
FAMILY

chapter four

ECOLOGY OF THE CANTICLE OF CREATION

Saint Francis and the life sciences agree—Earth's creatures live in dynamic relationship with each other. The *Canticle of the Creatures* sings of creation as a familial, interdependent system. All elements have a particular role, all are related, all play a part. Biology and ecology confirm this through scientific means. For most of the twentieth century, biologists described nature as "red in tooth and claw," as shaped primarily by relationships of competition and predation: It was eat lunch or be lunch. Recent scientific discoveries have highlighted the relationships of mutual interdependence, even cooperation among different species. Ecology makes this clear: Life is diverse, interdependent and vulnerable.[1] Saint Francis celebrated these spiritual insights centuries before biology or ecology were developed. He recognized creation as good, lived out conscious relationships with elements and creatures and expressed compassion toward them. His example inspires us to care for creation today. This chapter describes the diversity of life, also known as biodiversity, and how we humans are woven into life's fabric. It then offers a portrait of the *biodiversity crisis,* a new term to describe the full scale of species extinction. It concludes by proposing a Franciscan response to the biodiversity crisis based on a vision of humans as brothers and sisters to all creation.

OF RABBITS, WORMS AND CRICKETS

Biodiversity should have a special importance in Franciscan spirituality because of the importance of diverse creatures in the life of Francis. The early stories of his life relate more than a dozen encounters with rabbits, worms, lambs, fish and crickets. Birds appear most frequently in these stories, and Francis referred to them as noble creatures. Unfortunately, popular stories of Francis' relationship with animals have been "domesticated" and rendered quaint. The common image of Francis and the birdbath is a case in point.[2] A close analysis of these stories, however, indicates that unlike other medieval saints, Francis was profoundly affected by his encounters with creatures.[3] The story of Francis preaching to the birds illustrates this point well. Most modern people are tickled to discover a saint that preached to creatures, but the most important lesson from this encounter is related after he preached to the birds and they flew away. Thomas of Celano wrote, "After the birds had listened so reverently to the Word of God, he began to accuse himself of negligence because he had not preached to them before. From that day on, he carefully exhorted all birds, all animals, all reptiles, and also insensible creatures, to love the Creator, because daily, *invoking the name* of the Savior, he observed their obedience in his own experience."[4] Roger Sorrell argues that this experience served to integrate Francis' care for creatures with his understanding of himself as preacher, and that it resulted in a "new outlook" on creation.[5] The most important part of this story is not that he preached to birds but the impact that preaching to birds had *on him*. After his encounter with the birds, he "woke up" and recognized that they were his brothers and sisters as well. In the same way we may ask, how do we relate to this richly diverse Earth as brothers and sisters?

•

DYNAMIC ECOSYSTEMS

The *oikos*, God's house, brims over with a rich diversity of life. All creatures need food, a home and a family. Ours is not a homogenous, monotonous home planet, no, for it offers an abundance of food sources, diverse habitats and vibrant ecosystems. The diversity of environmental conditions offers a multiplicity of diverse strategies for organisms to make a living; thus, the diversity of life. But ecosystems are so dynamic that each creature can reshape them and allow other creatures to make their living, and further diversify life in that ecosystem. For example, after a wet winter, a pond or small wetland develops. Migratory birds carry in seeds for specialized, water-loving plants from their droppings. Some insects are attracted to the wetland for food or shelter, which in turn attract insect-eating birds, who may find the right conditions for nesting. As this shows, soil and water alone do not define ecological niches. Life depends upon many factors.

Several examples illustrate how humans benefit from life's diversity. The lowly earthworm, picked up from the road by Saint Francis, helps humans by tilling the soil.[6] Their tunneling opens up air passages, helps the soil hold the right balance of water and allows microscopic creatures to convert rock and organic matter into fertile soil. Earthworm castings provide terrific natural fertilizer, which provides nutrients and energy for other decomposers. Worms are among the largest of soil creatures, and they help make the right conditions for the formation of topsoil. Organic farmers evaluate soil health by the number of earthworms they find in it. Food for humans depends on healthy soil, so we benefit from the work of earthworms. Our lives depend upon life's diversity.

Agriculture would collapse without the pollination work of bees, whom Francis praised for their hard work.[7] Many plants depend upon insects to fertilize their flowers. These plants have evolved the ability to produce proteins in their pollen, attracting bees. As they move from flower to flower, bees (and some other insects) transfer a portion of the pollen to other flowers, fertilizing them. Some plants and pollinators have evolved quite closely. For example, several species of desert cactus are utterly dependent upon one species of bat to pollinate its flowers— only at night! And one species of bee has evolved so that its specific vibration stimulates the tomato flower to release its pollen. Relationships like these are said to be tightly coupled, or *coevolved*.

As winter gives way to spring, a thousand-mile-wide green wave rolls across the deciduous forests of eastern North America. With the right temperature conditions, forest trees break bud and sprout leaves. Because these new leaves are at their most tender stage, insects emerging from hibernation flock to eat them. Many species of small birds follow this wave, living off the abundance of insects attracted to the green wave. The birds are in no way conscious of the service they provide the trees, but that does not stop the trees from benefiting from them. These are examples of *mutualism,* or a mutually beneficial relationship.[8]

God must delight in diversity, for creation certainly abounds with it. Taxonomy is the science of classifying organisms, and a *taxon* is a particular category of organisms sharing a common ancestry. A *species* is the fundamental taxon, for only members of that group are capable of viably reproducing with each other in nature. Evolutionary biologists trace the evolution of life from monera (such as bacteria) through protista (such as algae) to the higher kingdoms of plants, animals and fungi. In the seventeenth century a scientist estimated the number of species to be twenty thousand. This number proved to be far too small, yet even with all our scientific technologies today, we still have only identified a fraction of the diversity of life.

In fact, taxonomists are unsure even about the number of species we have actually identified, because they cannot agree on the numbers of species in some families of lesser-known creatures. For example, estimates of the numbers of mollusks range from 45,000 to 150,000. The best guess for the number of currently named and identified species on Earth is 1.9 million, give or take 100,000! Although one entomologist proposed the number of Earth's species to be as high as 30 million, scientific consensus has converged around an estimate of 12.5 million total species. Thus far, humans have been able to name less than one-sixth of life's diversity! More than 85 percent is yet to be identified, even with all our scientific knowledge. The most common plants and animals have been identified, and most of the yet-to-be described creatures are members of the monera, protista and fungi kingdoms.[9]

The diversity of life is greater than human understanding. When most people think of biodiversity, they tend to think of beautiful, large animals, trees or fish. In reality, insects are the most abundant taxon. They constitute about 56 percent of named species, followed by fungi at 8 percent. Biologist E.O. Wilson refers to insects as "the little things that run the world," because they play an essential role in shaping the organization and function of ecosystems, even though they are often invisible to the untrained eye. Vertebrate animals, those with a backbone, constitute less than 0.4 percent of named species, but of course, panda bears, whales, bald eagles and the like capture the popular imagination. Ecologists refer to colorful, attractive animals as "charismatic megafauna." On one hand, popular interest in these is good because this can stimulate biodiversity conservation initiatives. For example, concern over the possible extinction of the bald eagle, the United States national bird, led to passage of the United States Endangered Species Act. On the other hand, large and beautiful vertebrates can divert our gaze from the overall importance of the integrity of creation. The problem with charismatic megafauna is that public attention and funds follow them, but not the less visible, attractive or inspiring creatures, nor the unglamorous but critical work of protecting their habitat. Efforts to save charismatic megafauna are good, but will not succeed without a broader understanding of the Earth's biodiversity and the actions necessary to preserve the integrity of ecosystems upon which they depend.[10]

•

Habitat Conservation Is Vital

Human society also depends upon the health of ecosystems and biodiversity. "Ecosystem services" are the benefits to human society from the environment. Clean water, fertile soil and pollination of native and agricultural plants result from the service of creatures in their ecological niches. Wetlands and forests depend upon clean water. Wood and paper depend upon forest health. Marine fisheries depend upon clean coasts and oceans. These are goods that most humans take for granted.[11] The richness or number of species is the most visible—but not the only—dimension of biodiversity. This term also encompasses the diversity of microscopic genes and far-reaching ecosystems necessary to support the diversity of species. Preserving the diversity of life requires habitat conservation. If a species loses its habitat, or even if its ecological niche changes in subtle but biologically important ways, it may not survive. Many migratory songbirds are threatened by loss of habitat due to forest fragmentation in the United States and Central America. Even if 90 percent of a songbird's habitat along their migration route is intact, the 10 percent that has been lost may serve as the "weakest link," and threaten the viability of that species. If a population of species falls below a certain threshold, it does not have sufficient genetic variability to cope with environmental change. For example, some species of whales have been hunted virtually to extinction, but because of conservation initiatives, their populations have recovered somewhat. Will these species have sufficient genetic diversity to be able to respond to global climate change and its effect upon the oceans?

Recently, ecologists have begun describing the "biodiversity crisis," or the massive wave of species extinction now occurring. Ecosystems around the world are suffering from degradation due to human activities, and this is pushing many species to the brink of extinction. The International Union for the Conservation of Nature organizes global information about the biodiversity crisis, and its 2006 report documents the accelerating rate of extinction. Of the 40,000 species assessed, over 16,000 are at imminent risk of extinction, and that number is rising rapidly.[12] Birds and amphibians are among the taxa most at risk.

Habitat loss is the primary cause of species' extinction. Much habitat has been plowed, paved, clear-cut, dammed or drained. Some habitat is degraded by air or water pollution. For example, frogs and other amphibians across the world are declining, and many are approaching extinction. Although the scientific explanation for this is not entirely clear, it appears that industrial and agricultural chemicals are able to harm them—through their permeable skin—far more than other species. Some forms of pollution are invisible. Slight changes in the chemistry or even temperature of lakes and streams can push amphibians to extinction. If pollution is out of sight, it may be out of human minds, but it can continue to harm our bodies and other creatures.

Global climate change now looms as perhaps the greatest threat to the diversity of life, upsetting even the most remote habitat: Polar bears are poised to become one of the most visible casualties of melting ice caps. Climate change can serve to "evict" a species from its ecological niche by altering temperature and precipitation, making it inhospitable for species that had traditionally occupied that niche. Through global commerce or simple carelessness, human beings have moved many species to new habitats and, in some cases, new, more aggressive species have pushed threatened species to extinction.[13]

Direct taking of species—harvesting or hunting—is the most visible form of biodiversity loss and the most significant factor driving a few species to the brink of extinction. For most of human history, the oceans were thought to be limitless, and we fished as though they had an unlimited supply. Industrial fishing technologies are now so powerful that they strip everything out of the sea. In very poor countries, some fishermen are so desperate for any kind of fish that they use dynamite and cyanide to stun their prey. These crude technologies poison other creatures and destroy coral reefs, which are essential for the reproduction of future fish. This kind of myopic, unsustainable behavior is clearly foolish, yet the economic opportunities for impoverished people are so bleak that they have few other options. A very similar set of issues affects tropical forests: They were once thought to be limitless resources for timber, but are now groaning under human industrial exploitation, and very poor people in developing countries also exploit forests in a short-sighted way because they have so few economic options.

Two Conventional Ethical Approaches

Over the past few decades, many religious people have begun to recognize the ethical dimension of environmental issues, and many religious leaders and organizations are speaking out on behalf of the integrity of creation. This new effort, known as the "greening of religion," marks a new stage in the dialogue between science and religion. Rather than quarrel over the exact process by which the world was created, religious and scientific leaders are tackling the moral problem of the human destruction of creation. As partners they are challenging the contemporary view that the Earth exists only to serve human needs, and they are using ethics language to do this. The greening of religion is taking place in virtually every religious tradition across the globe, and addressing the biodiversity crisis has received a great deal of attention.[14]

Faith communities bring a most important resource to environmental concerns: the practice of communal ethical reflection. This is a most important contribution, for until recently, environmental concerns have been defined as scientific (by scientists) or as government policy problems (by activists). The environment has generally not been framed as having moral significance, although this is beginning to change. Among faith communities, the simple shift in language from "environment" to "creation" indicates that the Earth is not passive or morally neutral, but rather sacred and signals that it belongs to God. Let us examine three simple ways of organizing ethical thought about the integrity of creation.[15]

The first ethical approach can be summarized as an adaptation of the Golden Rule: Do unto the earth as you would want done unto you. Do not pollute drinking water, because someone will have to drink it. Do not pollute the air, because someone will have to breathe it. Do not fish out all the species in the ocean, because future generations will need them to feed themselves. In this context, the diversity of life is only valued for its benefits to us: It feeds us, provides us fiber or pleases us with its beauty. Although the adoption of this rule would mark progress in some areas, this is not a particularly mature approach because it carries forward an attitude of human domination that the Earth really only exists for humans. The emphasis on managing resources solely for human benefit is consistent with utilitarian, capitalist economics. It does not reflect a biblical or Franciscan view of creation nor an ecologically informed understanding of our planet.

The second approach has emerged as Scripture scholars and theologians have recognized the creation accounts of Genesis chapters one and two as laying the foundation for a stewardship ethic in Judaism and Christianity. Their most important contribution has been to challenge conventional interpretations of God granting human beings dominion over the Earth. Genesis 1:28 reads: "God blessed them, and God said to them, 'Be fertile and multiply, and fill the earth and subdue it; and have dominion over the fish of the sea and over the birds of the air and over every living thing that moves upon the earth.'" The word *dominion* has a very different connotation today, in our scientific industrial society, than in the ancient Near East. God's dominion over all creation, and our human dominion over the Earth is to echo the love, care and responsibility that God has toward the created world. God's dominion is founded upon love and justice; it could not be exploitive or abusive. The same special concern that God has for the poor, the immigrant, the widow and orphan extends to the vulnerable members of creation. Many Jews and Old Testament scholars now recognize that Genesis, the Torah and the Psalms speak of God's care for all creation, of which human beings are but a part. Humans have been accorded special gifts, but also special responsibilities to care for the Earth as God cares for it. If we believe that God's love is reflected in creation, how could we fail to safeguard it? Christian environmental ethics rooted in Genesis emphasize responsibility: We are given the duty to care for creation. It does not belong to us. The Earth is the Lord's and we must steward it on God's behalf. This was a consistent theme in the environmental teachings of Pope John Paul II.[16]

Stewardship ethics obligate people of faith to learn the basic elements of ecological science, for we cannot discharge this responsibility in ignorance. We must be able to use our human intelligence to make better decisions. Ecology is particularly helpful for this task because it helps us to recognize relationships and to learn from previous mistakes. For example, in the region of Yellowstone National Park, historical prejudice against large predatory animals resulted in hunting, trapping and killing wolves to the point of removing them from the ecosystem. Over the past century, ecologists noticed that the aspen groves in the park were in serious decline, due to herds of elk grazing them. About a decade ago, wolves were reintroduced to the system, and aspen groves began to regain their health. How did this predator, eating only other animals, help trees? The region already had grizzly and black bears, so what did the wolf add? Neither bears nor coyotes were able to run down elk herds, but packs of wolves could. Once wolves were reintroduced, elk returned to their migratory behavior. They continued to eat aspen, but for shorter periods of time. The introduction of wolves appears to be helping the bears as well. Once wolves chase down and kill an elk, the slower-moving bears amble up to the carcass and chase off the wolves. These creatures relate to each other in their ecosystem, and any effort to steward them without acknowledging that would fail. Even though these kinds of decisions are made by expert scientists, they cannot be implemented without public support.[17]

Few Americans today serve as land managers, so our options for expressing stewardship ethics are largely limited to the economic and political spheres of our lives: what we buy and the quality of our civic participation. Choosing to purchase environmentally friendly food, fiber and forestry products is one way to express concern for protection of the diversity of life. Making careful choices in what we buy, and most importantly, learning how to live a fulfilling life with less consumption, is the single most important way an individual can express a Christian stewardship ethic. Yet helping our civic communities and public agencies make better environmental decisions, especially with industry, land and resources, has the potential to have a far greater impact. Individuals can make a difference, but groups of individuals speaking in concert to economic, political and social leaders have brought about the most important environmental benefits.

•

FRANCIS' HUMBLE APPROACH

The third Franciscan approach to care for creation expresses Francis' practice of humility in a way that neither utilitarian nor stewardship ethics do. Francis was a brother to all creation; he was not a steward. He did not view elements or animals as something for which he was responsible but rather as brothers and sisters to which he related. Francis rejected power, ownership and authority for himself. He wanted to be humble, to live in solidarity with creation just as Christ did through the Incarnation. Francis recognized Jesus as "brother" through his shared humanity with others and thus his shared corporeality. His encounter with animals provoked a greater consciousness of his vocation of brother to all creation. Francis lived out of a horizontal, not a vertical, relationship with the earth. He manifested a familial or kinship ethic. He did not speak of stewardship, of being in charge, of being responsible, or of managing creation. Francis and Franciscan theologians describe the Earth and its diversity as sacramental. Life on Earth has intrinsic value because it is created by God, not merely because of its economic worth. The vast majority of species, in fact, serve no genuine functional purpose for humans. What value does a "useless" creature have in modern society where everything has a rank according to its economic worth? If an endangered species has no economic value, who will speak on behalf of its survival? Yet in the Franciscan tradition, creation has integrity and intrinsic value not because of its "worth" but because it is a reflection of God. Francis was not a practical man, and if we fully mimicked his approach, we would not have agriculture—or modern society. But his example reminds us that our first calling, our first responsibility, as human beings is to be creatures of God, living in relationship to Creator and creation. Our fundamental ethic is to love God and the rest of creation, and our stewardship responsibilities flow from that. For too long, modern society has emphasized the special privileges of humans, and so Francis' example reminds us of our essential creaturehood. He reminds us of our identity as human beings, members of and coparticipants in creation.

What, then, does the biodiversity crisis say about us as humans and our understanding of God as Creator? How can we humans, as one kind of creature, push so many other creatures of God to extinction? Why are we as a species unraveling the integrity of creation? At its deepest root, our ecological crises derive from our belief that humans are somehow above or fundamentally distinct from—indeed, absolutely superior to—the rest of creation. This conceit is incompatible with a Franciscan worldview.

•

WHAT IS OURS TO DO?

Francis observed God's creatures, and learned from them. From the birds, he realized that he had the responsibility to preach to them, to care for them, to share his essential identity as creatures of God with them. From the earthworm, he learned humility. He lived simply and close to the soil and the earth. From the bees he learned community, conviviality. He praised their hard work and their cooperative living. Francis understood himself as brother to all creation. If we understand our identity to be that of sister or brother to all creation, what do we need to do?

A Franciscan identity should give rise to a particular consciousness and ethical concern. Together these can help us deepen our spirituality of our Sister Mother Earth. First, we have to recover our ecological niche, our role in creation, based on our identity as "in-relationship-to" the rest of the Earth. We must develop greater awareness of the choices we make that harm the Earth and its creatures. These choices are individual and social. Making choices to simplify our lives, to lessen our use of resources, is fundamental to developing a Franciscan ecological consciousness. The United States has the highest rate of resource consumption on Earth, so in our household choices we carry power to express concern for creation on a daily basis. But ultimately, we can make a greater impact by engaging others. Franciscan spirituality is a common project, lived out in relationship to other humans and creatures. Francis can inspire us to speak on behalf of God's other creatures, to take action to protect their habitat and to promote policies that protect the integrity of life on Earth.

Learning how to live in relationship is fundamental to following the patron saint of ecology. Francis was open to relationship, to receiving from all, whether leper, human brother and sister, worms, birds, bishops, water, fire, wind or Blessed Mother Earth. Francis recognized the Incarnate Word of God in all living creatures. His openness meant he could recognize the blessing of being brother to all, and his response was humility. He did not practice domination or authority but sought to live as cocreature. He bore the pain of the world in his heart, and in this way, he followed in the footprints of his Lord.

NOTES

[1] Ecologists speak of ecosystems as having resilience. Ecosystems must generally undergo significant stress before they break down, but human-caused degradation is pushing many to the point at which they are vulnerable to collapse.

[2] Keith Douglass Warner, O.F.M., "Get Him Out of the Birdbath!" In *Franciscan Theology of the Environment: An Introductory Reader*, Dawn M. Nothwehr, O.S.F., ed. (Quincy, Ill.: Franciscan, 2003). Republished from "Out of the Birdbath: Following the Patron Saint of Ecology," *The Cord* 48.2 (March 1998): 74–85.

[3] Thomas of Celano, "Hagiographic Method in Reading Franciscan Sources: Stories of Francis and Creatures in Thomas of Celano's *First Life* (58-61)," *Greyfriars Review* 4.3 (1990).

[4] Thomas of Celano, "The Life of Saint Francis," 58, in *FA:ED*, vol. 1, p. 234.

[5] Roger D. Sorrell, *St. Francis of Assisi and Nature* (New York: Oxford University Press, 1988).

[6] James F. Edmiston, "How to Love a Worm,"in *Franciscan Theology of the Environment*, p. 388.

[7] Thomas of Celano, "The Life of Saint Francis," 58 in *FA:ED*. vol. 1, pp. 234–235.

[8] For background on biodiversity, see Edward O. Wilson, *The Diversity of Life* (New York: W.W. Norton, 1992) and *The Future of Life* (New York: Vintage, 2002).

[9] Biodiversity data in this section is taken from Michael J. Jeffries, *Biodiversity and Conservation* (London: Routledge, 1997). See also Jonathan E.M. Baillie, Craig Hilton-Taylor and Simon N. Stuart, eds., *IUCN Red List of Threatened Species: A Global Species Assessment* (Gland, Switzerland: International Union for the Conservation of Nature, 2004).

[10] Edward O. Wilson, *The Future of Life*, Edward O. Wilson, *The Creation: An Appeal to Save Life on Earth* (New York: W.W. Norton, 2006).

[11] Ecological Society of America, "Ecosystem Services: Benefits Supplied to Human Societies by Natural Ecosystems," *Issues in Ecology*, No. 2, Spring 1997, and Gretchen C. Daily, ed., *Nature's Services, Societal Dependence on Natural Ecosystems* (Washington, D.C.: Island, 1997).

[12] International Union for the Conservation of Nature, *Release of the 2006 IUCN Red List of Threatened Species Reveals Ongoing Decline of the Status of Plants and Animals* (news release, Geneva, Switzerland, 2006). For background on the concept of biodiversity, see David Takacs, *The Idea of Biodiversity: Philosophies of Paradise* (Baltimore: The Johns Hopkins Press, 1996).

[13] For an introduction to the environmental problems of invasive species, see Roy G. Van Driesche and Jason Van Driesche, *Nature out of Place: Biological Invasions in the Global Age* (Covello: Island, 2004). This is a huge and growing—and largely ignored by the general public—driver of the biodiversity crisis.

[14] Biodiversity Project, *Ethics for a Small Planet* (Madison, Wis.: Biodiversity Project, 2002). Roger S. Gottlieb, *A Greener Faith: Religious Environmentalism and Our Planet's Future* (Oxford: Oxford University Press, 2006).

[15] James B. Martin-Schramm and Robert L. Stivers, *Christian Environmental Ethics: A Case Method Approach* (Maryknoll, N.Y.: Orbis, 2003).

[16] Drew Christiansen, S.J., and Walter Grazer, eds., *And God Saw That It Was Good: Catholic Theology and the Environment* (Washington, D.C.: United States Catholic Conference, 1996).

[17] Douglas W. Smith, Rolf O. Peterson, and Douglas B. Houston, "Yellowstone After Wolves" *BioScience*, April 2003, pp. 25–40.

[chapter five]

CREATION AS FAMILY

About a year before he died, Francis stayed in a small hut behind the convent of San Damiano. His eye condition had deteriorated to such an extent that he could not tolerate daylight, so he had to stay in the darkness of his cell. One evening while reflecting on all the troubles he was enduring, Francis prayed "*Lord...make haste to help me* in my illnesses, so that I may be able to bear them patiently."[1] Upon which he heard,

> Tell me, brother, what if, in exchange for your illnesses and troubles, someone were to give you a treasure? And it would be so great and precious that, even if the whole earth were changed to pure gold, all stones to precious stones, and all water to balsam, you would still judge and hold all these things as nothing, as if they were earth, stones and water, in comparison to the great and precious treasure which was given you. Wouldn't you greatly rejoice?[2]

Francis answered, "Lord...this treasure would indeed be great, worth seeking, very precious, greatly lovable, and desirable."[3] The Lord responded to him, "Then, brother,...be glad and rejoice in your illnesses and troubles, because as of now, you are as secure as if you were already in my kingdom."[4] The next morning Francis awoke and composed the *Canticle of the Creatures* so that God would be rightly praised throughout all creation.

THE CANTICLE OF CREATION

Francis' *Canticle of the Creatures* is a song of creation. It is a melody of brotherhood and sisterhood in a harmony of all creatures. We could easily read this hymn as a beautiful piece of poetry from a great Italian saint or we can find comfort in its balance of gendered life in the universe. But the *Canticle* is more than poetry; it is the work of a mystic, arising from a spiritual depth of love. It is the song of living in the family of creation. In the *Canticle* we see that nature has meaning in itself because it is created by God, as Eric Doyle notes, not because its value or meaning is given to it by humans.[5] To appreciate what the *Canticle* can teach us, we must touch upon its God-centeredness, as it flows from an inner source of love.

Bonaventure reminds us that creation emanates from the mouth of God who speaks a Word of love. This Word transforms what is nothing into something that lovingly reflects the heart of God. Creation is the eternal generation of the Word from the Father. The self-communicative love of the Father is literally God giving Godself away, but in such a way that marks the Trinity's dynamic, eternal life. Just as the Word is the inner self-expression of God, the created order is the external expression of the inner Word. Creation expresses the thoughts or ideas of God and therefore is a book by which we can know God. God, who is the purest of love within, creates not out of any need but out of desire to manifest something of the mystery of the divine truth, goodness and beauty outwardly and to bring forth creatures capable of participating in the splendor of the divine life.[6]

•

THE MYSTERY OF THE TRINITY AND THE *CANTICLE OF THE CREATURES*

Trinity and creation are related in such a way that creation is not brute "matter" but is the living Word of God expressed in a rich diversity of living creatures. Creation is not a mere external act of God, an object on the fringe of divine power; rather, it is rooted in the self-diffusive goodness of God's inner life and emerges out of the innermost depths of

Trinitarian life. To say that creation shares in the mystery of the Trinity means that it is caught up in the dynamic process of self-transcendence and self-communication of relationships and creative love. What characterizes the inner life of God, therefore, dynamic relationships of love, takes place in creation as well. God creates the world as the Father begets the Son; indeed, creation is co-spoken in the Word that is the Father's self-utterance and co-loved in the Spirit breathed mutually by the Father and the Son.[7] The reason for creation, therefore, lies entirely in the mystery of God, who is self-originating and self-communicating love. Creation expresses who God is as love. Since God's love can only be expressed in the divine Word, creation is a finite expression of the eternal Word of God. Such expression, however, does not diminish the one self-communication of God, the love of the Father for the Son in the spirit. Rather, God loves the world with the same love with which God eternally is.

The inner positive relation between the world and Word means that we know the world through the Word of God, and we know the Word of God through the world. That is why Christ is key to the truth of creation because Christ is the Word of God incarnate. In his life of Francis, Bonaventure shows that as Francis deepened his life in Christ, he came to know the truth of reality as the expressive Word of God's love. Growing in love in union with Christ led Francis to embrace creation as family. Through union with Christ, Francis stood in the midst of creation as a brother and, in turn, all of creation spoke to him of Christ. The three words of the *Canticle* that disclose the hymn as a cosmic Incarnation are the first and last words: "Most High" and "humility." These words express Francis' understanding that, in the Incarnation, the Most High God humbly bends down and enters into our weak, fragile human nature. A second key to the cosmic Incarnation of the hymn is Francis' address to "Sir Brother Sun": "Praised be You, my *Lord*, with all *Your creatures*, especially Sir Brother Sun." In his "Letter to the Faithful" Francis refers to Christ as our "brother and son": "Oh how holy and how loving, gratifying, humbling, peace-giving, sweet, worthy of love, and above all things desirable it is to have such a Brother and such a Son: our Lord Jesus Christ, Who laid down His life for His sheep."[8] Just as the physical sun is the center of our solar system and radiates light, so too the Son of God, Jesus Christ, is the center of our lives and radiates light.

The *Canticle* is infused with the mystery of Christ. A lifetime of following the footprints of Christ led Francis to proclaim the universe as the mystery of Christ. Francis' whole interiority, having been conformed and transformed in Christ, became like the alchemist's gold. With the impurities of his sinful self distilled, the *Canticle* revealed his inner life expressed as one with the universe in Christ who is the center of all reality. The *Canticle* shows an aesthetic appreciation for the things of creation delicately unfolding itself, born from the womb of the sacred.[9] It arises from a deep spring of inner joy in Francis. The *Canticle* discloses Francis' view of nature as a sacramental expression of God's generous love. This love binds us together in a family of relationships that are rightly termed "brother" and "sister." Through his love of Christ crucified Francis came to see the truth of reality, namely, that nothing exists autonomously; rather, everything is in relation to one other.

If the *Canticle* speaks to us of creation as family, it is because the notes of brotherhood and sisterhood resound harmoniously throughout it: brother wind, sister stars, Sister Mother Earth all remind us that we come from the fountain of the Most High, the Father's overflowing love, which flows through the Word into creation. "Humanity is creation become conscious of itself," Eric Doyle writes. "The human voice, therefore, speaks on behalf of all that is created."[10] The words "brother" and "sister" were words of mystery for Francis, because they so graphically disclosed to him the structure of reality. The reverence and love he had toward creatures evoked a response in them. Thomas of Celano recounts how Francis preached to the swallows and they recognized his affection for them and felt his tender love for them.[11] Love is the bond that impelled Francis to see every creature as his brother and sister.

In his *Major Legend of Saint Francis,* Bonaventure used the word *piety (Pietas)* which means "blood-related" or "family-related" to describe Francis' sense of relatedness to the family of creation. The word *piety* can be defined as an attitude of respect toward those to whom one is bound by ties of religion, consanguinity; of relationships between human beings.[12] Francis came to realize his "family" relatedness to everything, including the tiny creatures of creation through deep, interior bonds of love. "True piety," Bonaventure wrote, "had so filled Francis' heart and penetrated its depths that it seemed to have claimed the man of God completely into its dominion. This is what, through devotion, lifted him up to God; through compassion, transformed him into Christ; through self-emptying, turned him to his neighbor; through universal reconciliation with each thing, refashioned him to the state of innocence."[13]

Bonaventure contrasts the piety or family-relatedness of Francis to the impious or those who inflict cruelty on nature. He describes impiety, for example, in the killing of an innocent lamb: "Let human impiety pay attention to how great a punishment might at least be inflicted on it, if such animal cruelty is punished with so horrible a death." He contrasts such impiety with the *piety* and compassion of Francis who would not harm another creature because he was related to it as brother: "Let also the devotion of the faithful weigh how the *piety* in God's servant was of such marvelous power and of such abundant sweetness that even the nature of animals acknowledged it in their own way."[14] Bonaventure highlights what Francis professes in the *Canticle,* namely, that humans who live in unrelatedness (that is, sin) do not live in harmony with creation because they live over and against creation. Those who live in piety, however, live in relation to creation as family because they live with a sense of deeply rooted connectedness.

•

FRANCIS AND HIS APPRECIATION FOR DIVERSITY

To live in the family of creation, as Francis did, requires a sense of respect, appreciation for diversity and a willingness to share. It means being less self-centered ("it's all about me") and more concerned for the welfare of others. Such selfless concern did not happen quickly for Francis since he, like all humans, was marked by a gravity of self-centeredness. Francis strove wholeheartedly, however, to live a God-centered life through a life of penance. His piety was the fruit of his ongoing conversion. Growing in union with Christ through the Spirit gave Francis a new relationship to new nature, one in which grace and innocence prevailed, not sin and conflict. As his body became more in harmony with his spirit, and his spirit with God, he found that the created world provided for him, and he recognized others as fellow creatures and signs of Christ. Thomas of Celano wrote: "That the bees not perish of hunger in the icy winter, he commands that honey and the finest wine should be set out for them.... He calls all animals by a fraternal name, although, among all kinds of beasts, he especially loves the meek."[15] Francis' attentiveness to the weak and fragile in nature and his compassion for all creatures showed that he stood in creation as a "lesser brother," one who was humble and poor and thus dependent on the goodness of God, wherever that goodness was encountered in creation.

Francis showed deference to the elements of creation. The notion of *cortesia* or deferential behavior characterized Francis' respect for creation, including the natural elements such as fire. Thomas of Celano recounts the story of Francis' cauterization for an eye disease. To prepare the iron instrument for treatment, the physician had to place it in the fire until it became red hot. Francis apparently panicked and spoke to the fire: "My brother fire, your beauty is the envy of all creatures, the Most High created you strong, beautiful and useful. *Be gracious to me in this hour;* be courteous! *For a long time I have loved you* in the Lord. I pray the Great Lord who created you to temper now your heart that I may bear your gentle burning."[16] While we might find this deference toward nature exaggerated, Francis' respect for creation was not a duty or obligation but arose out of an inner love by which creation and the source of creation, namely God, were intimately united. Francis' relatedness to all creatures gave new meaning to the Lord's Prayer, the Our Father, which was the first prayer he taught the brothers to pray. Doyle claims:

> The *Our Father*, then, becomes the prayer of all creatures in the universe to their Creator and Father in the sounds produced in the human respiratory tract which we call words. Whatever God may have to forgive the rocks, the leaves, the flowers, the swallows, the foxes, earth, air, fire and water, there is no doubt how much they have to forgive us when we pray: "Forgive us our trespasses as we forgive those who trespass against us."[17]

Do we ask forgiveness of the Earth we have plundered? Francis' sense of solidarity with all creation reflected his connection to the web of life. We are realizing, in light of evolution, that each beginning of finite life is an insertion into the web of life; thus, the entire web changes with each new addition of created being or life. In this way, the "self" is not a substantive part within an individual but a pattern of relationships that is formed and influenced by the relationships themselves.[18] Every human interaction, therefore, contributes to our sense of self in one way or another and embodies a type of mutual power that allows for transformation of self through internal relations.[19] Francis grasped the need for relationship as the realization of selfhood. And he was not selective, for his relationships included birds, rabbits, earthworms, bees, flowers, trees and many other living creatures. Finding himself as a member of the large and diverse family of creation, Francis lived as an "ecological self" or a self inserted into the web of life. Just as his "The Praises To Be Said at All the Hours" included "every creature *in heaven, on earth and* under the earth,"[20] so too he directed the Our Father to the total love of God and forgiveness of sin. Praying for daily nourishment through the life of Jesus Christ and for the forgiveness of sins, especially between humans and non-human nature, can bring a spiritual power of healing and reconciliation to the broken relationships in creation, in which God dwells in faithful love.

Returning the Favor

The *Canticle* reminds us that we humans are as dependent on the elements of creation as they are dependent on us. With his marvelous respect for creatures of all kinds, for sun, moon, stars, water, wind, fire and earth, Francis came to see that all creation gives praise to God. Brother Sun and Sister Moon praise God just by being sun and moon.[21] Brother wind and sister stars praise God by being wind and stars. Francis developed a deep sense of universal community because Christ became the center of his very being through the power of love. Love enabled Francis to let go of control and to allow that which exists to be itself, and in that being to realize the radiant goodness of God. Love gives being to being; it gives more being to what is loved so that what is loved can become truly what it is. Such love is the fruit of contemplative union with God but not a union exclusive of God. As we see in the life of Francis, union with God is union with all other beings, whether humans, animals, plants or the elements. There can be no true love of God without true love of all creatures; thus, full union with God must include all creation. Eric Doyle says:

> To love is to be in relation with another, creating a bond between the self and a part of the world, and so ultimately between self and all creation. If one person can love one other person, one unique animal, one flower, one special place on this earth, there is no reason in principle why that love cannot stretch out to embrace every single creature to the furthest reaches of space.[22]

There is no doubt that Francis discovered his interrelatedness to the cosmos through compassionate love by which he came to experience a unity of all things in Christ.

Peace is the fruit of love, and Francis lived peacefully in the family of creation. After he had composed the first part of his *Canticle*, a conflict arose between the bishop and mayor of Assisi. Although Francis was ill, he was moved to help the situation and intervened by composing a verse of praises, included in the *Canticle:* "Praised be You, my Lord, through those who give pardon for Your love, and bear infirmity and tribulation. Blessed are those who endure in peace, For by You, Most High, shall they be crowned." To be a peacemaker is to accept the gift of peace given to us in Christ, a gift that flows out of the wounds of the crucified Christ. To accept this gift, we must accept our own woundedness and then acknowledge our wounding of others, including the trees, the forests and rivers and all creatures of creation. The love that brings peace is accepting woundedness or sacrifice *for the sake of others*, ultimately, loving others by way of self-gift.[23]

Francis believed that peace begins in the heart. "As you announce peace with your mouth," he said, "make sure that you have greater peace in your hearts.... Let everyone be drawn to peace and kindness through your peace and gentleness."[24] Yet he recognized that violence also begins in the human heart because the heart joined to the will has the freedom to choose to love or not to love. Peace is not just the absence of conflict or the tranquility of order, but the peace the gospel speaks of; peace at the core and center of one's being. Francis' simple act of praying with attention, turning his mind and heart to God, helped him grow in awareness of who God was and who he was, and in this awareness he found the energy of transformation both for himself and the world around him. Such awareness lessened his need for frantic control and manipulation. He accepted himself as part of the problem of sinful humanity and strove to realize his dependency on his brothers and sisters and all of creation.

In the *Canticle* Francis speaks of peace only *after* he sings of the harmony of brotherhood and sisterhood with the cosmic elements. Creation is "reconciled space," Kathy Warren claims, and "is in relation as brother/sister."[25] Humans do not appear in the first nine verses of the *Canticle* because they do not enjoy this harmony. We might say that humans live in the space of sin and thus separation. They live in division with each other and with nature. When they do appear, it is in the context of pardon and reconciliation. Humans are part of the harmony of creation only when they pardon and bear their sufferings, that is, when they can live in a spirit of love that can bridge the distance between divisive persons or between humans and creatures. To be part of the song of creation is to pardon, forgive and accept the weaknesses of others by allowing them to be what they are and loving them as they are. Forgiveness is an excess of goodness given to another for the sake of a new future. This superabundant goodness bridges the separation between human persons or between persons and nonhuman creation. Those who follow the path of peace and reconciliation are liberated from the blindness of heart and can see the presence of the Most High in the simple things of creation.[26]

Peace and reconciliation require a depth of love and it is the centrality of love that leads Francis to address "Sister Bodily Death" in the last part of the *Canticle:* "Praised be You, my Lord, through our Sister Bodily Death, from whom no one living can escape. Woe to those who die in mortal sin. Blessed are those whom death will find in Your most holy will, for *the second death* shall do them no harm." Francis' tribute to death, calling it "Sister," was composed shortly before his own bodily death in 1226. However, he prefaces bodily death by extolling a first death, saying that "for those who endure a first death, the second death shall do them no harm." What does Francis mean by this second death? All of Francis' life was a "death" we might say because it involved a continual "letting go" for the sake of the other, a constant "dying to self" so that Christ might live in him. Francis' "first death" is a death to the self-centered ego, the selfish-self who refuses the poverty of existence and the dependency on others, the isolated self who desires to exert itself through power and control over others. This self, in Francis' view, must die for once the self learns to let go of everything that prevents it from being its "true" self, it finds itself in a web of life, a family of creation. The second death, the death of the body, then becomes a complete participation in the cosmic community of life.

Francis' praise of death is a return of love for love. In his own way he tells us that the world is not blindly hurtling itself into extinction but is moved by Christ to Christ that God may be all in all. Perhaps Francis understood that what happened in the death of Jesus anticipated the future of humanity and the cosmos itself. The death of Jesus was not the annihilation of creation but its radical transformation through the power of God's life-giving Spirit. Jesus' resurrection is the beginning of the transformation of the world and this includes the world of nature. That is why in his sermon on the transfiguration Bonaventure could say *all things* are transformed and transfigured in Christ, for as a human being Christ has something in common with all things: "With the stone he shares existence; with plants he shares life; with animals he shares sensation; and with angels he shares intelligence. Thus all things are transformed in Christ since in his human nature he embraces something of every creature in himself when he is transfigured."[27]

But the path to transformation and transfiguration is through self-surrender; it is the path of the crucified Christ. It is giving up isolated existence for the sake of greater union. The death of Jesus is not the end of cosmic history but the beginning of union and fullness of life for all humanity and creation. Death is the passage into life's fullness. It is the tearing of the veil and the removal of boundaries that prevent us from engaging as relational beings in the unity of love. Death is the release into a deeper, more comprehensive relationship with the whole universe. The human spirit surrenders its limited bodily structure and becomes open toward the universe and, in some way, a true brother and sister to the elements of the universe. What we see in the life of Jesus and in the song of Francis is that God does not create for death, annihilation or frustration but rather to perfect his creatures unto fullness of their participated being. Just as the human person, soul and body will be transformed in the resurrection, so too will the cosmos. The whole universe is created by God for a purpose so that the whole created order will be brought into the glorification of the full body of Christ. All of nature is *cruciform*, Holmes Rolston writes, "this whole evolutionary upslope is a calling in which renewed life comes by blasting the old. Life is gathered up in the midst of its throes, a blessed tragedy, lived in grace through a besetting storm."[28] We are called to let go and enter into the storm, to love passionately and extravagantly as God has loved us. We are called into the fullness of life in the universe through the outstretched arms of crucified love.

•

SPECIAL RESPONSIBILITIES

Francis' *Canticle* reminds us that we are not called to relate to a God without a world. To love this God we must also love what God loves. The beauty of the present moment expresses the perfection of the eternal; however, beauty is revealed when we humans strive to make the right choices that correspond to a God who is infinite love. Since all of reality is good and beautiful, moral loving does not so much involve finding those objects worthy of love (since all reality is good) but rather working out the manner by which we can love reality as it deserves.[29]

Duns Scotus envisioned a harmony of goodness through the unity of love. My moral loving involves my relationship to all beings which surround me and my efforts to strengthen and enhance their mutuality. Like Francis, Scotus maintains that relationship is the key to the beauty of the universe. Since all reality is good, then my relationships with others, human and nonhuman, ought to promote goodness.[30] This is what justice is for Scotus, the orientation of rational beings toward right loving and right action. Justice is a stance toward reality. It involves treating everything in creation as it deserves. It calls us to attend to the "thisness," the inherent dignity of each and every thing that exists. When we act justly and love rightly, when we treat things with utmost dignity according to their inherent goodness realizing that each unique thing is singularly wanted and loved by God, then we help promote the harmony of goodness. This is the harmony of a diverse and created order in which the whole of creation gives glory and praise to God, the infinite, loving

Creator. Creation is charged with the goodness of God and, even in eternal life creation will sing the praises and glory of God. ❧

NOTES

[1] "The Assisi Compilation," 83, in *FA:ED*, vol. 2, p. 185.
[2] "The Assisi Compilation," 83, in *FA:ED*, vol. 2, p. 185.
[3] "The Assisi Compilation," 83, in *FA:ED*, vol. 2, p. 185.
[4] "The Assisi Compilation," 83, in *FA:ED*, vol. 2, p. 185.
[5] Cited in Roger Sorrell, *St. Francis of Assisi and Nature*, p. 123.
[6] Zachary Hayes, *Bonaventure: Mystical Writings* (New York: Crossroad, 1999), p. 112.
[7] Zachary Hayes, "The Meaning of *Convenientia* in the Metaphysics of St. Bonaventure," *Franciscan Studies,* 34, (1974), p. 89.
[8] Francis of Assisi, "Later Admonition and Exhortation," 56, in *FA:ED*, vol. 1, p. 49.
[9] Roger Sorrell, *St. Francis of Assisi and Nature*, p. 125.
[10] Eric Doyle, *St. Francis and the Song of Brotherhood and Sisterhood* (New York: Franciscan Institute, 1997), p. 77.
[11] Doyle, p. 76.
[12] According to the *Oxford Latin Dictionary*, the word *pietas* is defined "as an attitude of respect toward those to whom one is bound by ties of religion, consanguinity; of relationships between human beings: a. of children to parents, b. of parents to children, c. between husband and wife, d. of other relationships." See *Oxford Latin Dictionary*, P.G.W. Glare, ed. (Oxford: Clarendon, 1982), p. 1378.
[13] Bonaventure, "The Major Legend of Saint Francis," in *FA:ED*, vol. 2, p. 531.
[14] Bonaventure, "The Major Legend of Saint Francis," in *FA:ED*, vol. 2, p. 591.
[15] Thomas of Celano, "The Remembrance of the Desire of a Soul," in *FA:ED*, vol. 2, p. 354.
[16] Thomas of Celano, "The Remembrance of the Desire of a Soul," in *FA:ED*, vol. 2, p. 355.
[17] Doyle, p. 77.
[18] Kopas, *Sacred Identity*, p. 103.
[19] Kopas, p. 103.
[20] Francis of Assisi, "The Praises To Be Said at All the Hours," 8, in *FA:ED*, vol. 1, p. 161.

[21] Kenan B. Osborne, *The Franciscan Intellectual Tradition: Tracing Its Origins and Identifying Its Central Components*, vol. 1, Elise Saggau, ed. (St. Bonaventure, N.Y.: Franciscan Institute, 2004), p. 42.

[22] Eric Doyle, "The Canticle of Brother Sun and the Value of Creation," in *A Franciscan Theology of the Environment: An Introductory Reader*, Dawn M. Nothwehr, ed. (Quincy, Ill.: Franciscan, 2002), p. 160.

[23] This is Bonaventure's idea of perfect love as he describes it in his spiritual work, *The Triple Way*. See Bonaventure, *Triplicia via* 2.11 (VIII, 10), de Vinck, trans., "The Triple Way or Love Enkindled," p. 78. In his *Breviloquium* Bonaventure explains the order of charity as love of God, love of our self, love of neighbor equally as our self and love of body. See *Breviloquium* 5.8 (V, 261).

[24] "The Anonymous of Perugia," 8.38, *FA:ED*, vol. 2, pp. 52–53.

[25] Kathleen A. Warren, *Daring to Cross the Threshold: Francis of Assisi Encounters Sultan Malek al-Kamil* (Rochester, Minn.: Sisters of St. Francis, 2003), p. 99.

[26] Warren, p. 100.

[27] Bonaventure, *Serm.* I, *Dom.* II in *Quad.* (IX, 215-219) Hayes, trans. "Christ, Word of God and Exemplar of Humanity," *The Cord* 46.1 (1996), p. 13.

[28] Holmes Rolston III, "Kenosis and Nature," in *The Work of Love: Creation as Kenosis*, John Polkinghorne (Grand Rapids: Wm. B. Eerdmans, 2001), p. 59.

[29] Mary Beth Ingham, "A Certain Affection for Justice," *The Cord* 45.3 (1995), p. 17.

[30] Ingham, p. 17.

chapter six

EXPERIENCING THE KINSHIP OF CREATION

BROTHER TO ALL CREATION

The theologian Elizabeth Johnson, in a recent keynote address, recalled these words of the second-century saint Irenaeus: "*The glory of God is the human fully alive.*" She went on to say that "a stark sign of our times is the planet in peril at our hands."[1] In the midst of our current ecological crises, Johnson asks, might not Irenaeus's wisdom sound something like this? "*The glory of God is the earth fully alive.*" Surely, the harm we as humans are inflicting on nature (and, by extension, ourselves and each other) is a sign of neither the human nor the earth fully alive.

Thomas Berry claims that our modern-day task is to "reinvent the human—at the species level, with critical reflection, within the community of life-systems."[2] Our task is to learn to live within our humble place as part of—not superior to—our living planet. The guided meditation and subsequent activities in this chapter help to make real for us our participation in the diversity of life through our connectedness to the great web of life. The activities also help us to examine how our lack of realization of this interconnectedness has serious implications: We are tearing at the very fabric of life. A "Franciscan Ecological Examination of Conscience" is presented to encourage you to increase your awareness of the impact our lifestyles have on the magnificent biodiversity of life. Only through growing in awareness of our harmful relationship with nature will we be able to repent and amend our ways. "Listening to the Plight of Our Sister Mother Earth" is a group activity that offers a profound sense of the plight of endangered species, and a powerful understanding of our interconnectedness—through our destructive *as well as* our constructive actions—with the plight of all of creation.

Francis walked the earth with a unique sense of kinship with all the world. This sense of family flowed from his love of his Creator and, likewise, this sense of interconnectedness prompted him to live a life of penance. Only by rediscovering our essential creaturehood and our humble place within the web of life, and letting this transform our lives, will we be able to find the joy and freedom of being "humans fully alive." The magnitude of the changes needed to accomplish this task are daunting, but the reward great: We will discover our place in the harmony of creation that was God's intention and will be able to rejoice with an "Earth fully alive."

. . . .

GUIDED MEDITATION: CREATION AS FAMILY

(To prepare for the following meditation, please refer to Appendix B: Preparing for Guided Prayer Experiences. Once you have familiarized yourself with the format as presented, feel free to add different people or creatures to make the prayer experience more individually suited to you.)

As you begin your prayer time, find a comfortable position and close your eyes. Bring your attention to your breath and allow your body to relax. Simply notice your breath, with no need to change it in any way. When your mind wanders, gently nudge it back to the breath, letting it rest there as your body begins to relax. (Pause.)

Bring to your awareness the fact that your breath happens by itself, without any act of will. No decision to inhale or exhale is necessary to do this simple and life-sustaining act of breathing. It is almost as if you are being breathed, breathed by life.[3] (Pause.) Spend a few moments now, imagining yourself being breathed in this way—the Spirit moving through you in every instance, in a grace-filled act of replenishing each of your cells with oxygen, every moment of your life, whether you are aware of it or not. (Pause.)

Now bring your attention to other people around you—maybe in your house right now, or living in your apartment complex or neighborhood. They, too, are being breathed by life in this same moment. Let the faces of those you love—family and friends—slowly pass across your mind's eye. Wherever they are, whatever they are doing, they, too, are being breathed by life, by the Spirit that connects us all. (Pause.)

Imagine this circle of connection widening out, beyond your loved ones to others all across the city or town where you live…people driving and eating, people sleeping, reading, dancing, people enjoying a meal together or going to church; people giving birth, people dying; people laughing and people crying, people in hospitals and nursing homes, people in prison, people in villages, on farms, in great cities all over the world, people in war-torn villages, people all across the globe, sleeping on the other side of our planet, people just waking up as the Earth turns toward the sun—all of them are being breathed by life in this present moment. (Pause.)

Now extend your circle of care even further to include all of creation. Beginning with the mammals, bring to mind any pets you might have in your home. Remember, then, all the animals—squirrels, raccoons and moles; coyotes, bears and beavers; elk, cows, porcupines—and other animals in your ecosystem. These brother and sister beings, too, are being breathed by life today. With them, we are embedded in a diverse web of life that is greater than human understanding. (Pause.)

Now bring to your attention all the insects—bees, flies, gnats, dragonflies, lightning bugs, butterflies, spiders—all "the little things that run the world." Think of all the services they provide us—they who help pollinate the flowers and plants, who help break down waste, who enrich the soil—all of them playing crucial roles in the interconnected mystery of life on our planet. (Pause.) Bring to mind, too, the other winged creatures—sparrows, songbirds, great birds of prey. Bring them into your circle of awareness, all of God's creatures being breathed by life right now in this present moment. (Pause.)

Remember, too, the creatures living in the waters of our planet—fish, dolphins, whales, jellyfish and frogs, plankton and phytoplankton and all the microscopic creatures that float through our seas and make up the foundation of our food chain. We are all genetic kin in the great community of life that emerged from the ancient seas.[4] Give thanks for these creatures, part of the family of creation, also participating in the great breath of our world. (Pause.)

Widen your circle of awareness now to include that living mantle of vegetation that is home to millions of creatures across our globe. All the plants, flowers, trees, algae…they too take part in that great exchange of air, acting as the planet's lungs, constantly regenerating the entire atmosphere in the mutual dance of breath that sustains us all.[5] (Pause.)

We are connected through time and space with all of creation, and our home is within a dynamic, expanding universe. We are made of stardust, along with everything else in the universe. As humans, we have evolved the capacity not only to know, but to reflect on what we know. Through humans, creation has become conscious. (Pause.) Because we can reflect on our knowing, we can make choices and thus change the course of things. We can learn from creation how to love and praise our common Creator, and we can use our human voice to speak on behalf of all that is created. Directing our mind to our breath, even for a few moments, exercises that exquisite capacity for attention that comes with the precious gift of being human.[6] (Pause.) When our society would have us clench up in fear, the Spirit breathes in and out through each of us, reminding us of our inherent belonging in the family of life, allowing us to reconnect with our Creator at any time, in any place. (Pause.)

When you are ready, bring your attention back into this room, back to the sensations of the breath as it breathes in and out through you this mystery of life, remembering that it is always there, whether we are aware or not, to beckon us back to that connection with all of life—with this living planet, with our brother and sister creatures, bound together in God's love within the living canticle of creation. (Pause.) Pause to give thanks for this magnificent kinship of life that we have been given. Set an intention to walk as Francis did, more aware of the interrelatedness and sacramentality of all of creation as you move through your life today. In any moment, you can draw strength from the family of creation of which you are a part and bring this strength and wisdom into your daily life. (Pause.) When you are ready, open your eyes.

• • • • • • • • • • • • • • • • • •

A FRANCISCAN ECOLOGICAL EXAMINATION OF CONSCIENCE

Whatever God may have to forgive the rocks, the leaves, the flowers, the swallows, the foxes, earth, air, fire and water, there is no doubt how much they have to forgive us when we pray: "Forgive us our trespasses as we forgive those who trespass against us."[7]

Do we ask forgiveness of the Earth we have plundered?

Central to following in the footprints of Francis is living a life of penance. If it were easy to transform our lives to be in harmony with creation, we would have changed our ways long ago. It takes sacrifice and times of suffering to let go of habits that have become comfortable for us and that society tells us are our human right. Living a life of piety in the example of Francis means renewing our relationship with the entire created world and building lifestyles rooted in the knowledge that we are but one of the many valuable members within the family of creation.

Before we can transform our lives into ones of piety, we must look honestly at our lifestyles and see clearly how God is calling us to change. From within our Christian tradition, the examination of conscience is a means for doing this. The following is an adaptation of this ancient tool that has been designed to help us look at our lives within the context of care for God's creation.[8] To prepare to do an ecological examination of conscience, take a few minutes to quiet yourself and enter into a state of prayer. Going back over your day or week, ask yourself the following questions:

1. Is my whole life centered on God's overflowing love in my life, revealed through Jesus and through all of creation? Do I respond wholeheartedly to the call of this Spirit in my life?

2. Do I accept with a grateful heart the gifts of God's goodness and diversity in creation? Do I respond as Francis did, by building bonds of love, care, concern and companionship with all living beings? Do I value creation not as mine alone but first and foremost as God's home?

3. Am I willing to accept Francis' invitation to live as a "lesser brother or sister" within the kinship of creation? Do I pray for the forgiveness of sins between humans and the created world, and for the healing and reconciliation of our broken relationship with creation?

4. Am I caring toward my larger family of creation? Have I shown fidelity, humility, reverence and love to my Sister Mother Earth and all

my brother and sister species? Have I used my God-given gifts to honor and protect the diverse, interdependent, fragile nature of all life and to preserve it for all future beings?

5. Have I lived in a state of unrelatedness, over and against creation? Have I stolen from or damaged the habitat of other creatures by wasting or consuming more than I need, consuming virgin wood or fiber or choosing not to recycle and conserve? Do I share with all living beings that which God has given us all, or do I take the gifts of creation as my own? Does my lifestyle ensure that future generations will live in a world rich with the diversity of life?

6. Do I seek to eliminate from the world whatever keeps all creatures from their full development intended by their Creator: pollution, greed, overconsumption, loss of habitat, disease, war, extinction of species, oppressive laws and structures? Do I support organizations that work for ecological improvement on a systemic scale (not only for charismatic megafauna), restoration of habitat and preservation of open spaces?

7. Have I committed myself to follow Francis' example of ecological conversion? Have I encouraged others to take care for creation seriously? Have I been judgmental or mean-spirited toward myself or others when we live imperfectly in our journey to heal our relationship with creation?

After spending time with these questions, hold in your mind and heart the ways in which you have lived in disharmony with creation. Ask the earth and the Creator for forgiveness for your transgressions. Offer these mistakes up to God and ask for the strength and the wisdom to learn to live with integrity within the web of creation. Resolve to amend your life in the spirit of penance and love for our world.

MAKING ECOLOGICAL AMENDS: WHERE TO BEGIN

God's gift of peace is a gift graciously given through a form of love that is willing to undergo suffering. To accept this gift, we must accept our own woundedness and then acknowledge our wounding of others, including the trees, the forests and rivers and all creatures of creation. The love that brings peace is accepting woundedness or sacrifice for the sake of others, ultimately, loving others by way of self-gift.[9]

Completing an ecological examination of conscience can be a difficult task. One realizes even more clearly just how much our daily lives impact all of creation, by virtue of unconscious habits, but also because of the systems and institutions of our society that contribute to our destructive footprint on creation. Examining our conscience can be a first step toward becoming more conscious of our impact, and identifying steps toward living a more intentional life. It is also crucial to remember that making ecological amends means rediscovering relationship with others. We cannot expect to go about this business of changing such large-scale problems alone. We can be tempted to "go it alone" because we are taught to believe that we are isolated entities, separate from the rest of the world. Francis, again, can be our teacher here. He found solace and support in community as he strove to live out a life of penance and transform unjust structures in our world.

While it is good to recognize ways we are not living in right relationship with our world, excessive guilt or shame are not productive in motivating us to change our ways. Francis' respect for creation arose not out of duty or obligation, but instead flowed from knowing the abundant love of a generous Creator. Francis provides us an inspiring example of an engaged spirituality and reminds us that if we keep our lives centered on God, joy and freedom will flow as we transform our lives. We have all experienced moments of this, albeit fleeting at times. Take some time now to think of when you have made small choices to simplify your life and build community with others. Were there moments of joy and peace that flowed from that choice? The following simple points are helpful in taking the first steps toward amending our lives to begin to live again in right relationship with our world:

1. Simplify your life. There are many excellent resources for learning to live a fulfilling life with less consumption:

• Gather friends or form a group at church to discuss and reflect with a discussion course or book designed for this. Earth Ministry has published books and discussion courses such as *Simple Living, Compassionate Life, Food, Faith and Sustainability* and *The Cry of Creation: A Call For Climate Justice*[10] and the Northwest Earth Institute offers courses such as *Voluntary Simplicity, Choices for Sustainable Living, Healthy Children, Healthy Planet,* which give practical knowledge and ideas for action to reduce human impact on our planet.[11]

• Plan ahead and simplify the next holiday, family gathering, wedding or community celebration. The Center for a New American Dream[12] and Alternatives for Simple Living[13] have helpful guides for where to begin.

2. Build a supportive community. The web of creation reminds us that we are inherently interdependent! One of the most important ways to begin to build virtue and live a more ecologically aware life is to do it with others. Giving voice to your intention with others is a powerful way to hold yourself accountable, and community also provides creative ideas and much-needed support. Find a friend, talk to a spiritual director, or join with your faith community to support yourself in the transformative practice of making ecological amends and living a life of reflective action.

3. Take action in your community. Choose one of many local environmental issues related to biodiversity and habitat protection and inform yourself. Follow it in the newspapers and media for one month and then discern one action you can do to help your local or state government make better environmental decisions. Join with a sustainability group or simple living group in your area to gain support for taking action.

LISTENING TO THE PLIGHT OF OUR SISTER MOTHER EARTH

The following activity is a powerful, creative group process that builds solidarity with other species and elements in creation and a deep appreciation for what they have to teach us. It also allows participants to experience and grow their ecological selves, and to face not only the grief and destruction we as humans are causing other species, but also to discover the hope that comes when we take our proper place with the family of creation. This activity is an abbreviated form of the "Council of All Beings," which was created by John Seed and Joanna Macy.[14] While the original activity works best when you have a large group and several hours, this version is shorter and can be done with a smaller group.

This activity is based on the fact that, in our modern world, the nonhuman members of creation have no voice in the decisions, policies and practices that affect their lives and their home. Christians have a long tradition of being a loving witness for, and speaking on behalf of, the poor and the voiceless, but we seldom realize that all the creatures of our earth are truly among the marginalized.[15] When we have a chance to listen to our sister and brother beings speak about the things that most impact them, it can move our hearts and strengthen our connections with the family of creation. In this activity each group member allows themselves to "be chosen" by another life-form in creation. Using their imaginations, participants allow themselves to consider life from this being's perspective, and they speak for this being with their small groups. While grief and despair almost certainly arise during this activity, the strength and wisdom offered by our brother and sister beings also lends a sense of hope and support. Encourage the group to hold both sides of these feelings. Grief, anger, fear and discouragement are natural as we face the destruction of our home, and honoring those feelings will unblock our courage and hope as well.[16]

Begin by having your group break into small groups of four, and have them move their chairs into a cluster, facing each other. It is important that all the groups be the same size, and four works best in terms of time. The facilitators can join a group or not participate to even out the numbers. Have precut magazine or calendar images of a wide variety of animals, plants, mountains, lakes, trees and flowers spread out on a large table before you begin. When the small groups have set up their small circles, and everyone is ready to begin, have them leave their chairs for a moment to stand in a large circle around the table with the images. Begin by reciting a reading or song that invokes a sense of our interconnection with all creation, such as the *Canticle of the Creatures, Chief Seattle's Message*[17] or the song *Sacred Creation*. Group members should close their eyes as the group leader leads them through some simple breathing and centering, followed by this meditation:

• •

GUIDED MEDITATIONS: RECOGNIZING OUR BROTHERS AND SISTERS

Saint Francis was profoundly affected by his encounters with creatures. He allowed these encounters to truly influence him to the point that he "woke up" and recognized that they were his brothers and sisters as well. Today we will each have an opportunity to step outside of our normal human identity and use our imagination to more deeply connect with the many other beings on our planet. Each of us will take on the identity of a nonhuman brother or sister being. As we imagine life from their perspective, and speak of their concerns and their wisdom, we can increase our sense of kinship within all creation. Later in your small groups we will speak for this being or life-form, giving its unique message a chance to be heard in our world.

On the table are images of God's creation. Your first step is to choose an image for the life-form whose identity you will assume for the rest of our time together. I encourage you to approach this process with an open mind and heart, without trying to force anything to happen. As you silently walk around the tables and look at the images, think of it as the life-form choosing you. Be open to surprises, the brother or sister being that chooses you could be a form of plant or animal life or an ecological feature like a piece of land or a body of water. Often the first image that catches your attention is what is right for you at this gathering today; it may be a being you know nothing about, not even its name. Just relax and allow yourself to be chosen by the life-form that wishes to speak through you. (Pause.) Once you have been chosen, remain silent as you take the image with you to your chair.

• •

Participants return to their small groups. First the leader asks each person to briefly introduce himself or herself, in their new identity, to the group. Remind them to assume the voice of their new identity as they speak, for example, "I am Cedar and I speak for all the trees of the forest." After each group member has introduced himself or herself, each group decides who will share first. Referring to three questions, which are posted in a prominent place, the leader reminds the first person to answer all three questions in ten minutes, speaking from the voice of their new identity. It is best for the leader to give a time signal every three to four minutes, reminding them to move to the next question. When ten minutes have passed, the leader gives a time signal and asks the next person in the group to take his or her turn.

1. Describe what it's like to be this life-form or being, the powers and perspectives you are given, the relationships that nourish you and that you nourish in return.
2. Describe the changes and difficulties you may be experiencing now, due to loss of habitat, pollution, toxic dumping, drift nets, clearcutting, factory farming.

3. Since humans are causing these difficulties and abuses, and only they can correct them, consider what strengths of yours you can offer to the humans to help them make the changes necessary to your survival—and the survival of life on Earth.

After all four groups have shared, allow each group to express any last comments to each other. Then ask everyone to close their eyes and take a few deep breaths as they honor their beings one last time. Ask them to bring to mind the gifts of the experience and anything they learned or felt in the process. The leader can conclude this part of the exercise by reflecting that the gifts each life-form has given are already present within us by virtue of the web of life—otherwise they would not have occurred to us. Have them silently thank that being for the chance to speak for them in this activity. When they are ready, they can open their eyes. When the whole group has drawn together, people may share what life-forms spoke through them, and what they discovered in the process.

NOTES

[1] Elizabeth Johnson, "So Much is in Bud, How Can We Tire of Hope?" Keynote address at the Northwest Catholic Women's Convocation, Seattle, Washington, April, 2005.

[2] Thomas Berry, *The Great Work: Our Way into the Future* (New York: Bell Tower, 1999), p. 159.

[3] Joanna Macy and Molly Young Brown, *Coming Back to Life: Practices to Reconnect Our Lives, Our World* (Gabriola Island, B.C.: New Society, 1998), p. 190. This meditation borrows from Joanna Macy's original version as well as Carolyn Claire Mitchell's adaptation.

[4] Johnson.

[5] Michael Dowd, *EarthSpirit: A Handbook for Nurturing an Ecological Christianity*, 3rd ed. (New London, Conn.: Twenty-Third, 1992), p. 19.

[6] Joanna Macy, *Theory and Practice of the Work That Reconnects*, training intensive, August, 2005.

[7] Doyle, *Song of Brotherhood*, p. 77.

[8] Adapted from an examination of conscience used at St. Andrew Church, Portland, Oregon, Lent, 2002.

[9] Bonaventure, *The Triple Way*, p. 78.

[10] *Simple Living, Compassionate Life*, Michael Schut, ed. (New York: Living the Good News, 1999); *Food, Faith and Sustainability: Environmental, Spiritual, Community and Social Justice Implications of the Gift of Daily Bread* (Seattle: Earth Ministry, 1997). Earth Ministry also provides discussion courses, videos and resources for congregations in the area of care for creation. Contact them at 6512 23rd Ave. NW, Suite 317, Seattle, WA, 98117; http://www.earthministry.org/.

[11] Northwest Earth Institute provides excellent curriculum for discussion groups, and these courses are offered through sister institutes across the United States. Contact its main office at 317 SW Alder, Suite 1050, Portland, OR 97204; 503-227-2807; http://www.nwei.org/.

[12] Center for a New American Dream, "Simplify the Holidays," available from http://www.newdream.org/holiday/index.php.

[13] Alternatives for Simple Living, available from http://www.simpleliving.org.

[14] This is an adaptation of the Council of All Beings, described in Macy and Brown, pp. 161–165, republished from Seed, Macy, Fleming and Ness, *Thinking Like a Mountain* (Gabriola Island, B.C.: New Society, 1988).

[15] Thanks to Chris Peraro for this insight.

[16] For helpful tips handling strong emotions while leading group activities such as this, refer to "Guiding Group Work," chapter five, in Macy and Brown, pp. 63–80, or *The Work That Reconnects* (training DVD), available from New Society Publishers, 2007.

[17] One version of Chief Seattle's message can be found in Macy and Brown, p. 197.

•

•

•

•

•

part three

CREATION
AND
CONTEMPLATION

chapter seven

ECOLOGY OF THE *OIKOS*

Science is subversive. It challenges us to perceive the world in new ways. More than other scientific disciplines, ecology and the environmental sciences turn conventional human perception upside down. They challenge our human assumptions of being separate or apart from the rest of creation. Too many modern people assume that a great divide exists between humanity and nature, as if we did not depend upon the *oikos*, or that human actions could not seriously harm creation and ultimately ourselves. The science of ecology helps us recognize that humans are fully a part of creation, and that to believe we could ever live apart from it would be folly. The environmental sciences invite us to pay attention to our fundamental interdependence upon—and integration with—the *oikos*. Our human fate is inextricably bound to that of creation.

•

Understanding Our Global Climate

Planet Earth now faces an unprecedented threat: global climate change. This environmental problem challenges our ecological understanding as never before, because it defies traditional tools of conventional science. It poses a greater threat to the integrity of creation than any other human-caused environmental problem. Global climate change cannot be managed through conventional government regulation: It will require every person, every business and every institution to choose an alternative path if disaster upon disaster is to be avoided. It may pose the greatest threat to life on Earth that we have ever faced, and every future generation will be deeply affected by it. Ultimately global climate change is a theological challenge too because it requires us to reexamine our relationship with the Creator. This chapter will introduce the most basic elements of global climate science and its interpretation and then pose the question: How can we choose another path? And how can a contemporary Franciscan spirituality of the Earth help us discern an alternative path?

Earth is but one planet, yet because Earth is spherical, no one can ever see all of it at one time. Recent advances in the sciences allow scientists to measure changes on a global scale. Their findings point to the reality of the Earth as a complex of systems, or a system of systems. Few humans in contemporary society are even aware of how creation provides ecosystem services upon which our society depends. Sister Water comes to us through faucets. Brother Fire comes to us when we turn on the furnace or car. Our Sister Mother Earth comes to us through supermarkets. Yet Brother Wind comes to us unbidden! We have the least control over the air or weather. Scientific observation of the global climate has confirmed the interdependence of all systems of life. The energy and chemical flows described in chapter one weave humans and creation together more fully than we were aware, but in ways that are so complex that even the most sophisticated scientists strain to explain them. The full scale of this complexity still defies our human understanding, yet recent scientific research drives one point home: The fate of the Earth and the fate of humans is one. We depend upon the Earth for every aspect of life.

Take the simple example of breathing. We breathe repeatedly every minute, yet most of the time we do so unconsciously. As the previous chapter illustrated, breathing is not an isolated activity, but rather a practice that ties us ever more intimately with the rest of creation. There are several dimensions to our integration with the *oikos*. First, our bodies and the Earth's atmosphere are perfectly matched. We depend upon the air we breathe to have just the right blend of nitrogen and oxygen for our health. When air from the atmosphere enters our bodies, the boundaries between us and the rest of creation begin to blur. We draw oxygen into our body, where it enters our lungs and is absorbed by billions of red blood cells, which circulate the oxygen to our every cell. Simultaneously, carbon dioxide, a waste product in our bodies, is carried by the bloodstream back to our lungs where it is released as we exhale. If our lung surface is blocked by tiny particulate matter (soot, dust, pollution), we have difficulty breathing, and our body functions are thrown out of balance. A healthy life depends on clean air.

Second, the oxygen we breathe is not our own. We possess it for a short time, and then release it back to the rest of creation. Oxygen has been circulating through the environment since the beginning of life on Earth. Most atoms stay in our bodies for only a few years, perhaps as long as a decade. Each time we breathe in, we inhale atoms that have been a part of some other creature, whether tree, insect or animal. When we exhale, we release atoms that had been a part of our tissue, muscles or organs, and these flow out to be absorbed by other creatures.[1]

Third, we depend completely upon the plant kingdom for the oxygen they respire, for only plants convert carbon dioxide and water into oxygen (and carbohydrates). Their breathing complements ours, for they require what we release through respiration, and we breathe in what they exhale. Trees and plants also serve to cleanse or purify air from harmful chemicals. Yet we could also say that the Earth itself breathes. How is this?

Global climate science began when Roger Revelle proposed measuring carbon dioxide in the atmosphere, and he hired Charles Keeling to establish a monitoring station on the top of Mauna Loa, the highest volcano on the Big Island of Hawaii, beginning in 1958. Revelle noted that the economic expansion in the post–World War II years had resulted in a massive surge in the burning of fossil fuels, and he wanted to see whether he could track the carbon dioxide released into the atmosphere. Revelle and Keeling spent most of their professional lives studying atmospheric chemistry and its relationship to the Earth's ecosystems.[2] Keeling was the first to observe and record the annual fluctuations in carbon dioxide in the Earth's atmosphere and noticed a consistent pattern: Levels rise and fall by seven parts per million consistently throughout the year. Why is this? Notice the annual fluctuations shown in figure 2 and its inset. Throughout every winter leafless forest trees and plants respire carbon dioxide, pushing levels up. Every spring, a flush of new growth draws in carbon dioxide, and levels in the atmosphere decline. If land were distributed equally among the north half and south half of the globe, breathing by plant ecosystems would balance out, but most of the plant breathing occurs on land, and the Northern Hemisphere has more land than the Southern. This annual fluctuation was unanticipated by Revelle and Keeling. Imagine their surprise to find evidence of respiration on a global scale![3]

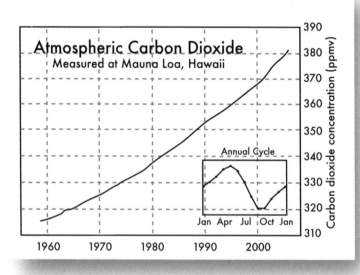

Figure 2. The Keeling Curve

But the most disconcerting information in the Keeling Curve is the continuous, upward trend in atmospheric carbon dioxide. Note that in the five decades since record-keeping began, the measured parts per million of carbon dioxide in the atmosphere has risen from 320 to 380, and the rate of increase is accelerating. Subsequent research demonstrated that human fossil fuel burning has raised the level of atmospheric carbon dioxide by roughly 30 percent since 1850. If this increase were to be charted over a longer time frame, say 2,000 years, it would be shaped like a sideways "L," or a hockey stick with the short piece curving up. It would show stable levels through the beginning of the twentieth century, followed by a steep increase, roughly keeping pace with the dramatic rise in human population and industry. The Keeling Curve is clear and undeniable evidence of human disruption of Earth's atmosphere. Christopher Uhl argues that this is the most important chart in the history of environmental science.[4] Yet carbon dioxide is "safe"—not toxic—for humans. We breathe it every day and have never thought of it as a pollutant. Why should we be concerned?

Revelle was motivated by concern that the increase in atmospheric carbon dioxide could seriously harm life on Earth. He undertook this project on a hunch, before he had scientific evidence of any impact or the tools to document it. Scientists have developed a powerful set of tools for describing the planet, its elemental components, living organisms and their relationships. They use the scientific method, a systematic approach to gathering information and determining facts. Thus, a scientific approach to studying the natural world asks questions, makes predictions (proposes hypotheses), tests the accuracy of those predictions and draws conclusions based on measurable evidence. Scientific investigations into global climate change have revolutionized our understanding of the fragility of the Earth's atmosphere, and the integration of the atmosphere with all aspects of life on the planet. Popularly referred to as "the greenhouse effect," "global climate change" is a more scientifically accurate term because it encompasses a cluster of changes in the Earth's climate, and not all of them involve making the Earth hotter. At first glance, the idea that humans could harm Earth's atmosphere seems preposterous. From the perspective of one individual person, the atmosphere is enormous, incomprehensibly so. From a global perspective, however, the atmosphere is quite thin, so thin that if you dipped a basketball into water and removed it, the film of water covering the ball would be proportionate to the thickness of the earth's atmosphere.[5]

•

GREENHOUSE GASES

We depend upon naturally occurring *greenhouse gases* every day to shield us from harmful rays from the sun and to contain sufficient heat in the atmosphere to support life. *Greenhouse gases,* such as carbon dioxide, methane, nitrous oxide and ozone, are components of the atmosphere that contribute to the warming of the Earth. The gases "trap" the heat radiated by the sun around the Earth—much like the glass panels in a greenhouse do—hence the greenhouse effect. The natural greenhouse effect is necessary for life to exist on Earth; in its absence the mean temperature of the Earth would be about 2 degrees Fahrenheit rather than the present average temperature of about 59 degrees Fahrenheit. Without the greenhouse effect, Earth would be as cold as the moon.

But scientific investigations into our climate have revealed the degree to which our human activities are disrupting its natural greenhouse effect. Our planet's climate has always been dynamic. The rate and degree of disruption caused by human economic activities is, however, without precedent. The following is a brief description of what scientists have discovered in their investigation into global climate change. Scientists discovered that the Earth's climate—and therefore climate science—is extraordinarily complex, far more so than initially realized. The industrial revolution (power plants, industry, transportation) was fueled by converting fossil carbon (coal, oil, natural gas) stored in the Earth's surface into energy. When fossil fuels are burned, they release energy and carbon dioxide. The increased levels of carbon dioxide affect the physical and chemical properties of the atmosphere, which is now trapping more solar energy than ever before. The increased solar energy within the atmosphere is fed back into our climate systems, which now behave differently.

Water is a peculiar substance, able to absorb tremendous amounts of energy. In the hydrological cycle, water circulates around the globe in our weather systems, evaporating from oceans, traveling in clouds and falling in various forms of precipitation, which ultimately return to the oceans. This water is now absorbing the additional solar energy captured by greenhouse gases. It appears that this solar energy is being released in larger and more destructive storms and hurricanes. These factors alter the dynamics of the Earth's water cycle, shifting rain and snowfall patterns and melting polar icecaps, glaciers and mountain snowpacks. Increased carbon dioxide reacts with other gases in the atmosphere to create carbonic acid, which is increasing the acidity of the oceans, thus affecting marine life. When polar ice melts, the reflective white changes to a more heat-absorbent blue (ocean) and gray (soil) and appears to be prompting rapid increases in temperatures, especially in the Arctic. This is called the *albedo effect*. The water released from the polar zones may change the dynamics of ocean currents, which have been relatively stable over recent history. Alterations in ocean currents will result in profound and dramatic shifts in weather patterns. These changes appear certain to raise ocean levels, flooding low-lying coastal areas. The above is merely a crude overview of the impact of global climate change.[6]

We should draw several critical conclusions from what is happening in the atmosphere. First, the four elements (air, earth, water and fire) are far more intertwined than we humans previously imagined. The changes we have made—and will continue to make—to the atmosphere have a cascade of impacts, just as knocking over one domino can result in many closely placed dominoes also falling. In scientific language, fire (energy), water and earth (soils) are tightly linked with the air (the atmospheric system). Because Earth's systems are so tightly coupled, global-scale disruption of the atmosphere will have cascade or multiplier effects across the planet, although precise details are difficult to predict scientifically. Complex systems with so many contingent interrelationships defy easy prediction. We can reasonably anticipate that the impact of dramatically increasing carbon dioxide will result in *nonlinear change*, or abrupt and unpredictable swings in rainfall, temperatures and ocean currents. Before the advent of global climate change, life was like walking a tightrope, learning how to maintain balance on a narrow rope as we ventured forward. In the era of global climate change, life will be like walking on a ball: Slight shifts in our balance can result in dramatic and unpredictable lurches, which can throw us off even more readily.

•

GLOBAL CLIMATE DISRUPTION

The amount of greenhouse gases we humans are emitting into the atmosphere, and the changes that is causing in our climate's behavior, are without historical precedent. The terms "greenhouse effect" and "global climate change" do not adequately describe what is happening. Human activity is disturbing our climate and the integrity of the planetary life support system. Thus, we are facing what should be called *human-caused global climate disruption*. Here are some specific concerns that scientists have raised. Even though climate change is a global phenomenon, most of the impacts will vary in different locations, frustrating efforts to predict them. Highly destructive storms, fueled by increased energy, will harm more areas of the world. If all glaciers on the Himalayan Mountains melt, the critical snowpack, which provides water for 40 percent of the human population, will be lost. Altered climate patterns mean that regions dependent on rain for crops and drinking water suffer severe droughts and agriculture may fail entirely in some countries. Dramatic changes in ocean chemistry could result in further loss of fish populations, upon which many poor nations depend for their food. Island and low-elevation nations are already experiencing the impact of rising oceans. Some islands in the Pacific Ocean have lost significant amounts of their land base. Some low-lying countries, such as

Bangladesh, already stressed by serious poverty and straining to feed their populations, will be inundated. Global climate change will adversely impact the other creatures as well. Ecosystems are highly dependent upon climate, and dramatic swings in weather will disturb habitats and accelerate the loss of species.

Global climate disruption poses a new kind of challenge to humanity. Unlike the visible effects of soot and smoke pollution, carbon dioxide pollution is invisible. It requires sophisticated scientific devices and expert interpretation to understand the changes we are making to our climate. The planet's atmosphere is so complex—contingent on the behavior of other Earth systems—that unraveling the cause and effect of the changes we are now seeing is very difficult. Experts disagree over the precise implications of the evidence. Earth's ecological systems are so complex as to frustrate definitive scientific prediction of global climate change. Yet if humans wait for evidence to emerge, the changes in Earth's climate will be so severe that it will be too late to avert global catastrophe. Thus, our fundamental challenge: Can humans act with prudence? Are we so committed to the current economic patterns of fossil fuel that we will endanger the future of humanity *and* the integrity of creation? Do we have the wisdom to recognize the warnings of scientists and chart an alternative course for positive change?

Global climate disruption is forcing human society to reexamine the relationship between science and faith. To date, human beings have been quite enthusiastic about using the fruits of science for economic prosperity and military might. We have not paid attention to the concerns raised by scientists about impending ecological problems. Many powerful economic and political leaders publicly question whether climate change is happening at all and have raised questions about global climate science. With anything as complex as the planet's atmosphere, scientists differ in their interpretation of the evidence. A decade ago some experts disagreed about the scope and threat of climate change, and the mass media and some people—deeply invested in our contemporary fossil fuel economy—have even manipulated scientific uncertainty to argue that we should not take action. The science of climate change is relatively new, less than thirty years old. As is often the case, scientists in this emerging field disagreed about many of its major components, but over the past decade, a broad consensus has emerged. A few scientists, funded by United States corporations economically invested in oil, gas and coal consumption, have set out to confuse the American public by claiming that the scientific community is deeply divided on this issue, when in fact there is near-unanimous consensus that ominous climate change is already underway. Scientists disagree largely about the severity and timing of the impact. The highest scientific authority in the United States, the National Academy of Science, joined with the national academies of science in nine other countries to affirm that climate change is real, to predict that serious consequences are already underway and to recommend that the governments of the world undertake major initiatives to reduce fossil fuel burning.[7] Evidence that global climate change is now already underway is overwhelming and irrefutable.

•

What Can We Do to Stop Global Warming?

How we Americans respond will say a great deal about our character and our values. The recommendation of scientists is simple enough: Reduce fossil fuel burning. Yet that will require a fundamental redesign of our entire economy to run on sustainable energy. Significant technological, policy and economic problems challenge the transition from a "carbon-based economy" to a sustainable energy economy. We have to begin dramatically restructuring our economic and technological systems now to avoid disruption. Yet a simple examination of other countries demonstrates the feasibility of this path and illustrates the isolation of American energy policy. As of this writing, every major country in the world has agreed to the Kyoto Protocol, the United Nations treaty that sets targets for reducing carbon emissions, with the exception of one: the United States. Most European countries are now undertaking major investments in alternative fuels to reduce carbon emissions and setting national targets for their reduction. These countries may be taking but incremental steps, but that is much more than the United States is doing. The United States leads the world in carbon dioxide emissions, roughly 30 percent of the planetary total, and we do not have any governmental plan or policy to reduce them. The United States government, acting on behalf of a few corporations, is the chief obstacle to addressing the greatest environmental threat humanity has ever faced.

As of this writing, however, some shifts in American public opinion are becoming discernable. Americans now recognize global climate change as a serious problem, and appear ready to participate in making changes. Yet to follow through on the difficult process of amending our ways, we will need courage and conviction to make sacrifices. Powerful political and economic forces will continue to deny human responsibility for disrupting Earth's climate, but it appears that a majority of people are interested in trying to be part of the solution. Yet the challenge of climate change is greater than any previous environmental problem we have faced because it suggests that we have to transition away from carbon-intensive fossil fuels, and this will require reengineering our entire society. The most profound impacts will not be visited upon our generation, but that of our children and grandchildren. This challenges us to focus on the virtue of prudence, on the practice of restraint in the present generation so that future generations can have a habitable planet. This will require us to move from fear for ourselves and our well-being to a stance of solidarity with others, in the present and future.

The risks to the future of life on Earth are frightening. To date, most Americans have responded to global climate change with denial, ignoring the problem or disputing the evidence. By itself, convincing people to be afraid of global climate change does not have sufficient power to transform our society and its inadequate understanding of creation.[8] This wall of resistance is beginning to give way, but we must be conscious that denial may turn into despair. Making the transition to a more sustainable energy economy is the solution to the crisis of global climate change. A truly frightening future faces the human family—indeed all of creation—if we cannot make this transition. Overcoming the fear and greed that paralyze us is only possible by entering more deeply into love and relationship with Creator and creation. Contemplative living is not merely an option to cope with fear. From a Franciscan perspective, it is the only real alternative that can make the Word of God alive in the world today. Contemplative living, rooted in a practice of prayer, will open up our hearts and minds to the turning, the repentance, the revolution needed to foster a more sustainable human society. The balance of this book will propose how we can respond creatively to our environmental crises by contemplative and compassionate living.

NOTES

[1] Christopher Uhl, *Developing Ecological Consciousness: Pathways to a Sustainable World* (Lanham, Md.: Rowman and Littlefield, 2004), pp. 93–101.

[2] Albert Gore, *An Inconvenient Truth* (Emmaus, Penn.: Rodale, 2006).

[3] Uhl, pp. 34-35; Gore; James Gustave Speth, *Red Sky at Morning: America and the Crisis of the Global Environment* (New Haven, Conn.: Yale University Press, 2004).

[4] Uhl, p. 34.

[5] This analogy and others about global climate change are from Uhl.

[6] For an introduction to global climate change, consult Uhl, Gore or Speth. For more scientific depth, consult the National Academy of Sciences Committee on the Science of Climate Change, *Climate Change Science: An Analysis of Some Key Questions* (Washington, D.C.: National Academy, 2001). Its report begins: "Greenhouse gases are accumulating in Earth's atmosphere as a result of human activities, causing surface air temperatures and subsurface ocean temperatures to rise.... most of the observed warming of the last 50 years is likely to have been due to the increase in greenhouse gas concentrations accurately reflects the current thinking of the scientific community on this issue" (1, 3).

[7] Joint National Science Academies, *Global Response to Climate Change* (Washington, D.C.: National Academy of Sciences, 2005).

[8] Michael Shellenberger and Ted Nordhaus, *Death of Environmentalism: Global Warming Politics in a Post-Environmental World* (New York: Breakthrough Institute, 2004).

[chapter eight]

FRANCISCAN CONTEMPLATION

In his book *Swimming in the Sun*, Albert Haase compares our search for God with the story of the little fish searching for water. Coming home after an exciting day at school, the fish exclaimed, "Mommy, they were talking about this thing called 'water' today in school. We swam all around looking for it—from the bottom of the ocean to the place where the land meets the sea—but couldn't find it! Where is this thing called 'water?'"[1] Oftentimes we are like the little fish in our search for God. We swim up and down the ocean of life looking for "God," completely unaware that we are submerged in the waters of God's love. How do we learn to feel and taste and touch this water of life? How do we awaken our senses to the overflowing goodness of God?

•

Holy Matters

Franciscan spirituality challenges us to recognize our capacity for relatedness. Do we know ourselves as relational beings and, if so, what do we see ourselves related to? Incarnation is the revelation of who we are at the source of our being—creatures of God—and who God is as the source of our lives and our world—the fullness of love. But do we really believe that God has entered into union with us and that this entire creation is integrally related to God? Joseph Chinnici, a Franciscan historian, claimed that "there has entered into our souls a deep prejudice against the Incarnation."[2] This is an alarming statement for Christians

123

because it says we deny the very thing we announce—intimate relationship with God. From where does this bias arise and how will it be overcome? Have we become modern Gnostics, believing that we will be saved by knowledge alone? Have our hearts and minds become permanently detached from each other so that we think without feeling? To live in relation to an incarnate God is to believe that matter is holy and that holy matter is the means to love God. Any relationship with God apart from matter is not Christian. That is why prayer and contemplation are essential to our lives, because only a life-giving relationship with God can sustain a life-giving Earth. Contemplation can strengthen our hearts, giving us courage to face the fearful effects we humans are having upon the Earth's life-support systems.

•

THE IMPORTANCE OF PRAYER

Prayer is subversive, and perhaps more subversive than science, for a person of prayer is one deeply rooted in the transformative power of God's love. Through prayer we come to perceive the world in new ways. Prayer helps us recognize that we humans (together with creation) have a capacity for self-transcendence. We are, in a sense, "wired for God." Prayer is that openness to God or, to use a modern term, "downloading" God into our hearts and minds. It is that breath of the Spirit that nurtures the roots of our lives. It is prayer that can change the way we go about in this creation because the Spirit creates a new heart within us and thus a new vision of the world. Francis did not so much pray, Thomas of Celano wrote, as he himself became prayer.[3] He became that living flame of God's love, visibly alive in the midst of creation. Francis learned to pray by detaching his inner heart from the lures of riches, fame, success and the pursuit of knowledge. Instead, he accepted poverty and humility, following Christ, as the path to life in God. Francis' life of prayer can be summed up in three short ideas: Let go, let be, let God be God. He strove to listen to the Spirit in his life and he followed the promptings of the Spirit, as he followed the path of Christ. His deep love of the Scriptures, his attentiveness to the Psalms and his love of the Eucharist all spoke of his inner grasp of the Incarnation as the humble descent of the Word of God into our midst. He had such a profound sense of God among us, in the weakness of human flesh and in the humble form of the Eucharist, that his life of prayer was an ever-deepening desire to see God, to know God and to love God. He repeatedly urged his followers to see God in the Body of Christ, in the poor and sick, who were mirrors of Christ, and in creation. Incarnation was so real for Francis that there was nothing profane in this world for him. Everything spoke to Francis of the living presence of God.

•

THE HEART OF FRANCIS

Francis was a contemplative person. Contemplation is a penetrating vision that gets to the truth of reality. Francis was a "heart-centered" person and throughout his life he strove for purity of heart. In his own writings he used the word *heart* forty-two times, compared to the word *intelligence,* which appears only one time, as does the word *intellect.*[4] The heart governed Francis' life. Through the eyes of his heart he saw creation, with the mind of his heart he sympathized with creation's weaknesses, and with the hands of his heart he felt the bonds of unity with all creatures. The heart of Francis brimmed with life because he came to realize that the entire creation is holy in and through his relationship with Jesus Christ. Wherever he went in the world, the arms of his heart were ready to extend themselves in love because the eyes of his heart saw the humble, overflowing goodness of God. Francis' prayer life led him to greater joy, to gratitude for creation, and to the practice of humility. It is "heart vision" that led Francis to contemplate the created world in its goodness and led him to take his place as one of God's creatures.

Francis came to realize that it is Christ who sanctifies creation and transforms it into the sacrament of God. The intimate link between creation and Incarnation revealed to Francis that the whole of creation is the place to encounter God. As his eyes opened to the holiness of creation, he came to see that there is nothing trivial or worthless in creation. Rather, all created things pointed beyond themselves to their Creator. Even two twigs crossed together reminded him of the cross. Wherever he went, into lonely wooded valleys or fields or hollowed-out caverns for prayer, he would bend low and kiss the ground saying, "We adore you, Christ, in all your churches throughout the world,...for by your holy cross you have redeemed the world."[5] Contemplation enabled Francis to "wake up" to the goodness of creation. His contemplative vision did not seek to change the world but to perceive creation as it truly is, rivulets of goodness flowing like a river from the mouth of the Most High. Francis came to "see" God in creation and love God through the things of creation.

•

BONAVENTURE ON FRANCIS AND CONTEMPLATION

Bonaventure describes contemplation as the union of knowledge and love, and thus a transformation into wisdom. Before the fall into sin, he said, humans stood upright in the garden of paradise and were able to contemplate the light of divine wisdom reflected in the mirror of creation.[6] Human beings were endowed with a triple eye: the eye of the flesh to see the world and what it contains; the eye of reason to see the soul and what it contains; and the eye of contemplation to see God and those things that are within God.[7] Throughout creation, the human person could discern the reflection of the Creator. Being made in the image of God, humans were oriented toward God through the gift of grace. The very nature of the human person, in Bonaventure's view, is to contemplate God because we are, by nature, oriented toward God. However, because of sin, humans became trapped in darkness and ignorance, causing them to lose the way to contemplate God. Bonaventure wrote: "As a result, [the human,] blinded and bent over, sits in darkness and does not see the light of heaven unless grace with justice come to his aid against concupiscence and unless knowledge with wisdom come to his aid against ignorance. All this is done through Jesus Christ."[8] Prayer is essential to restoring our full humanity because prayer seeks the grace that will bring the soul to the point where it is reoriented completely toward God.[9] "Just as no one comes to wisdom except through grace," he writes, "so no one comes to contemplation except by penetrating meditation, a holy life and devout prayer."[10] For Bonaventure, continuous prayer, purity of heart and desire for union leads the seeker of God to the contemplation of God.

In his *Soul's Journey into God* Bonaventure maps out the journey to contemplation through a unique synthesis of mystical theology, medieval symbolism and the example of Francis of Assisi. He begins on the level of creation with its order and beauty. Because creation speaks to us of God, it is a limited expression of God. By gazing on creation we are inspired to search inward for God, which leads us to self-knowledge and knowledge of God. We are led to consider the image of God in which we are created and, for Bonaventure, this consideration draws us into the mystery of Christ. As we ponder the mystery of God in Christ and the image in which we are created, we are led into the depths of the Trinity, the infinite communion of self-diffusive love. This ascent "upward" into the Trinity of love is one ultimately of the heart. Knowledge is important because we cannot love what we do not know; however, intellectual knowledge can lead us only to the doorstep of the Trinity. It is love that leads us into the heart of the Trinity. For Bonaventure, this love is the deepest knowledge of God.

Wisdom is knowledge deepened by love; it is an experiential knowledge of God. As the fullness of love, it is an interior affective "tasting" or delighting in the divine.[11] Wisdom is the vision of the heart whereby the heart sees the truth of things and thus knows in a way more deeply than the (intellectual) mind itself could ever grasp. It delights in God as good revealed in the interior of the soul. Wisdom is the gift of the Spirit given to one who has "passed over" into God; it is the fruit of union that leads to a proper relationship with God and creation. One who has arrived at a deep relationship with God, in which God's grace is predominate in one's life, arrives at wisdom because one's heart is no longer centered in "oneself" but in God. For Bonaventure contemplation is the fruit of union with the crucified Christ. "Contemplation cannot come about except in the greatest simplicity; and the greatest simplicity cannot exist except in the greatest poverty," he said.[12] Contemplation requires that we detach ourselves from everything that blocks God's presence in our lives—everything that obscures the vision of God—and attune ourselves to a wholehearted love of God.

For Bonaventure there is no contemplation without spiritual poverty, that is, without letting go of what we cling to in our lives, and acknowledging our radical dependency on God. Poverty is the first beatitude Jesus proclaimed on the Mount: "Blessed are the poor in spirit, for theirs is the kingdom of heaven" (Matthew 5:3). Poverty binds us to God and to one another; it is the sister of humility that respects the goodness of all created beings. Poverty can lead to contemplation when it leads to a union in love that is not afraid of suffering or "leaving behind oneself" for the sake of the other. It is giving up what we cling to for the sake of the earth and making room for its healing and wholeness. Poverty is the root of wisdom that sees the earth for what it truly is, the sacrament of God.

Contemplation is the fruit of union in love. It is the vision of the lover who gazes on the beloved. The biographers of Francis tell us that after he encountered the God of compassionate love in the visible figure of the crucified Christ, Francis' "vision" began to change. Prayer that leads to an openness of the Spirit and the indwelling of the Word (and Father) leads to an experience of penetrating vision by which one sees God in concrete reality. In Bonaventure's view contemplation bound Francis to the things of creation and opened his eyes to the truth of God in creation. He came to realize that the Incarnation sanctifies all creation. In Jesus not only does the fullness of divinity reside, but in him is subsumed all of creation as well. Earth, water, fire and air—the four cosmic elements—are not just God's creation; they are made holy by Jesus

Christ, in whom the elements of the universe are further sanctified.[13] As Francis' heart opened to the overflowing goodness of God, he began to "see" God's goodness incarnate—Christ—in every aspect of creation. Everything spoke to Francis of the infinite love of God. Trees, worms, flowers by the side of the road, all were for him saints gazing up into the face of God. Creation became the place to find God and, in finding God, Francis realized his intimate relationship to all of creation as a "brother." He discovered himself to be a member of the large, diverse family of creation.

Bonaventure describes Francis as a "contuitive person," who made of everything in creation a ladder by which he could climb up and embrace the Beloved. *Contuition* is a type of spiritual intuition, a depth of insight to what meets the eye. The notion of contuition pertains to the theologian whose task is to bring to light the depths of things in Scripture that both reveal and veil the divine mystery.[14] Bonaventure uses the word *perscrutatio,* which means "the action of uncovering, searching out, penetrating or fathoming," allowing the depth of the mystery to unveil itself without destroying it.[15] The theologian who is a *perscrutator* is like a treasure hunter or a seeker of pearls—she or he fathoms the unsuspected depths of the divine mystery, searches out its inmost hiding places and reveals its most beautiful jewels. Bonaventure indicates that when God expresses something of the divine Trinitarian grandeur, it is then left to the theologian to search it out or penetrate it insofar as one allows oneself to be inhabited by the wisdom of God, which alone brings all things to light.[16] To discover divine wisdom in this hidden order is not only to search the depths of God in himself but the depth of God hidden in God's created works in which and by which he justly manifests his wisdom. Francis was like a seeker of fine pearls, as he sought out the hidden presence of God in creation. In his life of Francis, Bonaventure wrote: "In beautiful things he contuited Beauty itself and through the footprints impressed in things he followed his Beloved everywhere, out of them all making for himself a ladder through which he could climb up to lay hold of him who is utterly desirable."[17] Francis saw God reflected on every level of creation, from stars to sun and moon to tiny earthworms and lambs, to his religious brothers and brother lepers. He discovered that the world is the cloister of God because each individual created thing bears a unique relationship to God and reflects the power, wisdom and goodness of God. He came to realize that creation is a *theophany,* or a revelation of God. Everything bows down before the divine, like the stars in Joseph's dream.[18]

Franciscan contemplation opens the heart and mind to take in more of the world, its beauty and suffering. Contemplative practice dilates one's heart, like a plant unfolding before Brother Sun's energy. It heightens our consciousness, our awareness of relationships with God and creation, strengthening our participation in creation, and the life of our Creator God. Francis lived in love and, by loving other creatures, let them be, encouraging them to grow in their uniqueness, sharing with them their very being. Bonaventure claims that Francis was moved with a sense of relatedness (piety) to all things.[19] He discovered that his life was incomplete without relationship to even the tiniest creatures of creation. Bonaventure writes that "he [Francis] would call creatures, no matter how small, by the name of 'brother' or 'sister' because he knew they shared with him the same beginning."[20] Everything in creation spoke to Francis of God. Just as he was impressed by the compassionate love of God in his encounter with the Crucified, so too he came to see that same love impressed on every level of creation. He found himself in a familial relationship with creation calling out to "Brother Lamb," "Sister Birds," and "Sister Cricket."[21]

•

THE WORLD PREGNANT WITH GOD

In Bonaventure's view Francis' depth-seeing was not merely a passive seeing but a deep penetrating gaze into the truth of the other, opening up his heart to receive the other in an embrace. In this way, the overflowing goodness of God permeating all of creation, first made visible in the beloved Christ, became visible in the disfigured flesh of the leper and the tiny things of creation. Francis' world was so imbued by the goodness of God that he was "aroused by *everything* to divine love." Bonaventure writes: "aroused by all things to the love of God, he rejoiced in all the works of the Lord's hands and from these joy-producing manifestations he rose to their life-giving principle and cause."[22] Thomas of Celano states: "Fields, vineyards, rocks and woods, and all the beauties of the field, flowing springs and blooming gardens, earth and fire, air and wind; all these he urged to love of God and to willing service."[23] Francis truly became a lover of God through the beautiful things of creation.

While Francis' nature mysticism may sound like a romantic story of medieval piety, there is a reality to his sense of relatedness. It can be summed up in one word: Incarnation. Many Christ-centered mystics, like Francis, have experienced the profound presence of God in creation. To know Christ in human form is to know God in created reality; to see God in the Eucharist is to see God in creation. The great penitent-mystic, Angela of Foligno, while attending Mass one day and seeing the host elevated, exclaimed:

> [I] beheld and comprehended the whole of creation, that is, what is on this side and what is beyond the sea.... And my soul in an excess of wonder cried out: "This world is pregnant with God!" Wherefore I understood how small is the whole of creation—that is, what is on this side and what is beyond the sea, the abyss, the sea itself, and everything else—but the power of God fills it all to overflowing.[24]

The idea of the whole earth "pregnant with God" speaks to us of "Mother Earth," a nourishing and caring Earth that cries out in labor pains, longing for its fulfillment in God (Roman 8:22). Angela's vision reminds us that the power of spiritual vision and relatedness is made possible by the power of love in union with Christ. To see God present with the eyes of the heart and to love what is seen requires faith in the risen Christ, truly believing that God is present to us in created reality. Do we really believe that God dwells with us, in our lives and in the natural world of creation? Does the Body of Christ move us to contemplate God in creation? If so, then how can we say "Amen" to receiving the Body of Christ and perpetrate destruction of the environment? There is a disconnect between what we claim to be or rather what we claim to see and what we actually do. It is an alienation of heart and mind that has rendered a desecration of the environment, as if we take the host, the Body of Christ, and continually stomp on it while saying, "yes, so be it!"

•

CLARE ON PRAYER AND CONTEMPLATION

How do we reconnect our hearts and minds to the Christ we claim to believe in? By learning to contemplate the presence of God in matter. Clare of Assisi offers some valuable insight with regard to prayer and contemplation. The path of prayer that leads to contemplation for Clare is not simply one of vision; rather, it is becoming what we see and love. Transformation of the human person is integrally united to the contemplation of God. We cannot contemplate God, she indicates, unless we are on the path of transformation. We contemplate God as we are transformed in God, or we might say, "we are conformed as we are transformed." Although the word "contemplation" literally means "one in mind with," for Clare the mind cannot be separated from the soul or from the heart. Contemplation, therefore, is of the mind, soul and heart and is a deepening of love through transformation in the beloved. Transformation is the basis of contemplation because only when the mind, soul and heart are open to the experience of God, touched by the grace of divine love, can one begin to contemplate God. Such change does not take place in isolation but in the encounter with God, as God comes to us in the person of Jesus Christ.

The way we begin to contemplate God for Clare is by learning to love the God who has descended to us in love, made visible in the cross of Christ. The cross is the mirror of God's love and the reflection of our own lives. In this mirror, Clare indicates, we begin to see who we are and what we are called to be. As we begin to pray in union with the crucified Christ, we begin to see who God is for us. Contemplation is the encounter with God as God appears to us in the ordinary flesh of our humanity. It is not a matter of introspection nor does it require a flight from the world. Rather, it is a penetrating gaze on the figure of Christ crucified and seeing there the presence of God.

For Clare, it is the eye of the heart that must learn to see rightly in the mirror of the cross. The progression of prayer that leads to contemplation begins with the gaze on the crucified Christ and continues to penetrate the depths of this reality until the margins of the cross, poverty and humility, give way to the heart of charity hidden in the heart of Christ. The movement toward contemplation is from outside to inside. It begins with the gaze of the Beloved on the cross, which leads to internalization of the Spirit that joins one to Christ. One is drawn into the mystery of God hidden in Christ. The path to contemplation is linked with the experience of fierce suffering, an experience of having to die. In some way one must experience a cleansing and purging of all that is not of God in order to live wholly centered in God. When someone has been purified intensely, the Beloved is experienced as the one "Whose affection excites / Whose contemplation refreshes / Whose kindness fulfills / Whose delight replenishes…."[25] We no longer live by our own strength but by the Spirit of Christ who works in us. For Clare, contemplation is entering a new place of refuge, the dwelling place of God's love. As a deepening of love, contemplation is a continuous action, an ongoing transformation, since nothing is more liberating and active than love. The contemplative not only sees the depth of things, but the vision itself also leads to a type of "felt-love," to compassion. Contemplation awakens the senses and brings them to a new level of openness to God. We see differently, hear differently, taste new things and touch the presence of God in what others perceive as profane reality. The contemplative realizes that there is nothing profane for those who know how to see.[26] Rather, one recognizes that we live in the ocean of God's love.

Contemplation is an indwelling in love that must ultimately lead to action because to love God is to see God, and to see is to act. It is a demanding type of vision because if we really see the truth of God hidden in the fragile things of creation, how can we turn away? Are we not impelled to reach out and touch this God we love? If we really see the depths of God revealed in persons or creatures who otherwise might be discarded, rejected or annihilated then we must act by a flame of love. We must do what we say we are—God-lovers. Clare realized that such action is not superficial; rather, it takes all that we are to unite with God in weak, fragile, suffering humanity. Contemplation, therefore, is joined to the cross. To see and to love what we see places a demand on our private, comfortable lives. We may be called to put our own agendas aside in order to care for another. Or we may be asked to sacrifice our goods for the good of the other. Contemplation is linked to costly discipleship; it is a renunciation of the claim "you're number one" because it sees there is another to love. There can be no "number one" where there is another human person or creature, for there is no "one" over the other, only a one that includes the other. Contemplation is the recognition that we are together in this oneness of life.

Francis tells us that contemplation is the work of the Holy Spirit. One must have the Spirit of the Lord, who joins one to Christ[27] to see into the depths of things.[28] This, too, is Clare's idea. Openness to the Spirit means a dynamic relationship with God. One who is joined to Christ has the spirit of Christ. It is the Spirit who opens the heart and mind to embrace the world in its beauty and suffering. The life of Francis shows us that contemplation does not necessarily mean optimism. Francis experienced tremendous suffering throughout his life. He confronted his fears of sickness and death and experienced profound darkness, which he overcame only with considerable struggle. He wrote the *Canticle of the Creatures* after he became blind, as he lay dying. He knew great pain but chose to embrace it and move through it toward participation in the life of God. Contemplation gave him the courage to do this. Whether surrounded by beauty or pain he contemplated the goodness of God. So, too, we can draw strength from contemplation to look boldly upon the state of the world. We must be able to perceive God's activity in the world first by seeing the goodness of God in ourselves, in the midst of our weaknesses and pains, and then to see God in the weakness and pain of the world. To love the God of compassionate love within us is to be moved to compassion for others and the creation on which we depend. Compassion is "the quivering of the heart in response to another's suffering."[29] It is the ability to "get inside the skin of another" in order to respond with loving concern and care. Compassion is so deep and closely connected to others that the truly loving person breathes in the pain of the world and breathes out compassion. The compassionate person identifies with the suffering of others in such a way that she or he makes a space within the heart, a womb of mercy, to allow suffering persons inside and to embrace them with arms of love. What we see in the life of Francis is that compassion begins with the God of compassionate love, for love is the power of God to transform what is dead into resurrected life. The power of God's love is not a power *over* the world but a power shown through the selflessness of the human person. It is the power of the contemplative who sees the dynamic interrelationship between God and creation, and thus who moves beyond the blindness caused by greed and selfishness to feel for the other and love the other, even at the cost of oneself.

The path to contemplation therefore begins with an acceptance of God's love in Christ, shown to us in the cross, followed by a continuous gaze into the truth of this love. As we come to dwell on the mystery of God's love for us, we come to a greater understanding of ourselves, who we are in relation to God. Only one who has a spirit of poverty can gaze long enough to become inwardly free to be joined with Christ. The gift of the Spirit is the fruit of poverty by which we are dispossessed of all the clutter in our hearts, becoming inwardly free to accept the embrace of God's love in Christ. The freedom that arises from poverty by which we allow God to be God is not a freedom *from* others but the freedom *for* others, including the creatures of creation. It is the Spirit who joins us to Christ and enables us to gaze into the heart of Christ. The contemplative person begins to see the God of humble love hidden in fragile, ordinary, created reality—the weak, the sick and the poor—and to love what one sees. Contemplation awakens one to gratitude for all that exists because every aspect of creation is a gift from a loving God. To see, to love and to become what we love is the fruit of contemplation that can only be realized when we accept the poverty of being human. Contemplation allows us to feel God's presence in our midst, to touch this presence and to taste its goodness. It gives us the ability to perceive more deeply, more fully, more completely ourselves—our bodies and senses, other persons, our neighbors, brothers and sisters, the ground on which we walk, the trees, plants, the sky and clouds, the sun and moon, all earthly creatures, everything visible and invisible. This kind of prayer helps us see who we really are as creatures of God. Through the doors of contemplation we are opened up to the mystery of God. That is why contemplation makes a difference in our actions. It gives us the courage we need to confront the impact we human creatures have on creation, to realize that our actions have eternal value and that we need selfless hearts rooted in God. Contemplation leads us into the mystery of God because it allows us to see and touch the depths of God. In this way, contemplation involves recognition of our fundamental relatedness to the whole, and unless we can find ourselves in solidarity with rather than in control of (or indifferent to) the whole, we risk global disaster.

Contemplation can nurture the vision of family in creation, helping us realize that we are all brothers and sisters to each other, and it can give us the courage to act on one another's behalf. We need the same depth of contemplation and compassion as Francis had if we are to confront our planetary environmental problems and our own instinctual fearful responses. How can we regain a sense of God-centeredness in our lives where we live with contemplative vision, where creation is celebrated as the pouring out of God's gracious goodness, where the inherent dignity of each living being is recognized and valued as expressing the infinite love of God? Can we begin to restore our hearts to see, to feel and to love by learning to contemplate God in creation? To see God outside ourselves we must first see God within ourselves. Contemplation dilates the inner eye of love by which we see who we are in God and who God is for us. Are we ready to see the truth in our midst? Are we ready to love for the sake of the whole? Contemplation opens us up to the truth that nothing in this creation belongs to us. That is why the contemplative falls to the ground and kisses it at the dawn of each new day, for the contemplative knows that creation is God's gifting us through the Trinity's delight of overflowing love. ✿

NOTES

[1] Albert Haase, *Swimming in the Sun: Discovering the Lord's Prayer with Francis of Assisi and Thomas Merton* (Cincinnati: St. Anthony Messenger Press, 1993), p. 16.

[2] Joseph Chinnici, "The Prophetic Heart: The Evangelical Form of Religious Life in the Contemporary United States," *The Cord* 42 (1994), p. 298.

[3] Thomas of Celano, "The Remembrance of the Desire of a Soul" in *FA:ED*, vol. 2, p. 310.

[4] Leonardo Boff, *The Cry of the Earth, The Cry of the Poor* (New York: Orbis, 1997), p. 209.

[5] Bonaventure, *The Major Legend of Saint Francis*, in *FA:ED*, vol. 2, p. 551. (Hereafter, *The Major Legend of Saint Francis* will be referred to as *Leg. maj.*)

[6] Bonaventure, II *Sent.* d. 23, a. 2, q. 3, concl. (II, 544b–545b). Bonaventure states that Adam was able to contemplate God without hindrance in the mirror of creation because the mirror was not yet obscured by the effects of sin.

[7] Bonaventure, *Breviloquium*, 2.12.5. Engl. trans. Monti, *Breviloquium*, p. 98.

[8] Bonaventure, *Itin.* 1.7 (297-298). Engl. trans. Cousins, *Bonaventure*, p. 62.

[9] Bonaventure, *Circum. Dom.* 1 (IX, 137a); *Comm. Lc* n. 15, c. 21–52 (VII, 389b–402a).

[10] Bonaventure, *Itin* 1.8 (V, 298). Engl. trans. Cousins, *Bonaventure*, p. 63.

[11] Bonaventure, III *Sent.* d. 35, a. 1, q. 1, concl. (III, 774b). Bonaventure puts forth a doctrine of the spiritual senses in his *Soul's Journey into God.*

[12] Ilia Delio, *A Franciscan View of Creation,* p. 12.

[13] Emmanuel Falque, "The Phenomenological Act of Perscrutatio in the Proemium of St. Bonaventure's Commentary on the Sentences," Elisa Mangina, trans. *Medieval Philosophy and Theology* 10 (2001), p. 6.

[14] Falque, "Phenomenological Act of *Perscrutatio,*" p. 9.

[15] Bonaventure, *Leg. maj.,* 9.1, *FA:ED,* vol. 2, p. 596.

[16] Hans Urs von Balthasar, *Studies in Theological Style: Clerical Styles,* Andrew Louth, Francis McDonagh and Brian McNeil, trans., vol. 2, *The Glory of the Lord: A Theological Aesthetics,* Joseph Fessio, ed. (San Francisco: Ignatius, 1984), p. 267.

[17] In his *Legenda major* Bonaventure states that "true piety filled Francis' heart....he was moved with piety to all things." See *Leg. maj.* 8.1 (EM, 64), *FA:ED,* vol. 2, p. 586. See also Bonaventure, *Leg. maj* 8.6 (EM, 68), *FA:ED,* vol. 2, p. 590.

[18] Bonaventure, *Leg. maj.,* 8.6, *FA:ED,* vol. 2, p. 590.

[19] Bonaventure, *Leg. maj.,* 8.6, *FA:ED,* vol. 2, p. 590.

[20] Bonaventure, *Leg. maj.,* 8.9, *FA:ED,* vol. 2, p. 590.

[21] Bonaventure, Leg. *maj.,* 8.9, *FA:ED,* vol. 2, p. 592.

[22] Bonaventure, Leg. *maj.,* 8.9, *FA:ED,* vol. 2, p. 593.

[23] Thomas of Celano, "Life of Francis," in *FA:ED,* vol. 1, p. 257.

[24] See *Angela of Foligno: Complete Works,* Paul LaChance, trans. and intro. (New York: Paulist, 1993), pp. 169–170.

[25] Clare of Assisi, "The Fourth Letter to Agnes," 11–12 (Écrits, 112). Regis J. Armstrong, trans. *Clare of Assisi: Early Documents,* p. 50.

[26] This is the insight of the Jesuit scientist and mystic Pierre Teilhard de Chardin. See his *The Divine Milieu: An Essay on the Interior Life,* William Collins, trans. (New York: Harper and Row, 1965), p. 66.

[27] Again, Francis gave primacy to the Spirit of the Lord as the one who makes life in Christ possible. In his "Later Admonition and Exhortation" he wrote: "We are spouses when the faithful soul united by the Holy Spirit to our Lord Jesus Christ." See his "Later Admonition and Exhortation," 51, in *FA:ED,* vol. 1, p. 49.

[28] The notion of penetrating vision is distinctive of Franciscan contemplation. Bonaventure used the term *contuition* to describe this penetrating vision, which sees a thing in itself and in its relation to God. For a more extensive definition of *contuition* see Ilia Delio, *Simply Bonaventure,* p. 199.

[29] Cited in Joyce Rupp, *The Cup of Our Life: A Guide for Spiritual Growth* (Notre Dame, Ind.: Ave Maria, 1997), p. 110.

[chapter nine]

CONTEMPLATING OUR CRUCIFIED EARTH

Contemplation is essential to understanding how to follow in the footprints of Francis and lead a life of reflective action. Contemplation in the Franciscan tradition is an essential part of an engaged spirituality; it asks us to really look at the world with seeing eyes. It involves withdrawing from the world in reflection, yes, but not to escape from the world or its problems. Rather, this stepping back offers a chance to take a penetrating look at the world *as it truly is*, in all its beauty and gift as well as its pain and injustice. Contemplation involves looking critically at the underlying structures of injustice and finding a way to be part of their transformation; it is anything that helps us to "unveil the illusions that masquerade as reality and reveal the reality behind the masks."[1] Yet contemplation also nurtures our spirit, and out of this inner fullness our actions become like a sacrament in this world—cocreating with God and making the spirit visible in our hurting world. Contemplation ignited Francis' heart, which led to his profound conversion and his commitment to living a penitent life. His kinship with all of creation was an occasion for joy, but it also brought with it grief and pain at the injustices suffered by that which he loved. This familial love for all of life ultimately compelled him to act with compassion and to promote peacemaking and justice in ways that often challenged the power structures of his time.

Looking at contemplation from this perspective, what does it mean for us as followers of Francis to take a contemplative approach to our modern-day ecological crises? If we dare to look and really see, we encounter Creation crucified—at our hands. This is truly a heartbreaking and terrifying reality, almost impossible to bear without the strong spiritual grounding that contemplation offers. If Francis were to walk our earth today, he would encounter for the first time his Sister Mother Earth, Brother Wind and Sister Water polluted and desecrated, the creatures he loved endangered and some gone forever. Francis never experienced this type of ecological devastation since it occurred largely after the Industrial Revolution, yet the way he lived his life can teach us how to contemplate such realities and then find the courage to act.

The story of Francis' encounter with a leper offers powerful guidance here. In his era, lepers were looked upon with scorn. They suffered intense social stigma, and their affliction was often seen as a punishment from God. In his youth Francis was no exception in his disdain for the lepers living on the outskirts of his town; in fact, he avoided them even more vigorously than others did. Perhaps their pain and disfigurement was too much for him to bear, so he assumed the cultural messages of his time, which helped justify this collective "looking away" of society from the lepers' plight. However, early in his conversion God's love shone through to Francis in his encounter with a leper, and it profoundly changed his life. Soon after he went to live with the lepers, caring for them as his own kin and experiencing true joy in this service. Francis' transformed heart was what made the difference; he saw in the leper's eyes that God "humbly bends low in love and hides in weak and fragile forms." This transformed understanding flowed from a heart that was grounded in love and the knowledge of his relatedness to his brother leper through their common Creator. How can contemplation help us do as Francis did—face harsh realities and injustices in our world despite the pain and discomfort we might experience in the face of that suffering? How can a contemplative heart help us to discover again our love for the family of creation and help us to find the courage to act in its defense? Like Francis in his encounter with the leper, we must learn how to gaze upon our damaged, disfigured and disregarded Earth with contemplative eyes, for when we hold within our hearts the pain of our world long enough for it to transform us, we discover the courage and hope needed to act on behalf of creation.

In the same way that Francis' fear and apathy caused him to shun the leper early in his life, we humans—in our collective inaction—shun our ailing Earth and the plight of all her living creatures. Why is this? What keeps us from taking action to heal our world? This chapter focuses on the some of the obstacles that prevent us from doing our part to care for our crucified Earth: denial, apathy, disempowerment and despair. In the guided meditation, the process of "breathing through" is offered as a practical tool to use whenever we encounter difficult feelings—from a disagreement with a friend to the powerlessness of the huge and complex ecological crises we now face. Individual actions are discussed that can help us to assess and begin the process of changing our individual contributions to global climate change: They begin to "lay the groundwork" for rebuilding the house of creation. Group reflection questions then encourage us to examine what prevents us from joining with Francis to "rebuild the *oikos.*" What are the challenges each of us face when contemplating difficult realities and the need to take action? The contemplative practices in this chapter prepare our hearts for embarking on the path of an engaged spirituality that interacts with our larger communities, which will be discussed in detail in section four.

Fundamental to the approach of many of the world's great spiritual traditions, and surely to Francis' approach to life, is the recognition that we are not separate, isolated entities, but are interrelated to all of creation. Our mechanistic society teaches us to view ourselves as isolated from the family of creation, and this strips us of the power and strength inherently found there. Because of our belonging in the great web of life, we can have confidence that we will discover an inherent resilience and support when we open to the pain of the world. Opening to the world like this, in all its beauty and pain, rather than shutting it out, enhances our awareness of our place in the family of creation, and our status as cocreators with God.

Joanna Macy, perhaps more than any other spiritual teacher of our time, has deeply discerned how our despair for the world contributes to our inaction in the face of pressing crises. She has developed a theoretical and practical framework for tapping into the resources of our spiritual traditions and learning how to face the painful realities of our ecological crises.

Her teachings are the source for many of the concepts introduced in this chapter. One of the methods she encourages people to use is the process of "breathing through," which can be practiced in any situation where we face difficult information or feelings, whether listening to the daily news, encountering another who is in pain or going through a challenging situation ourselves. The following meditation is only slightly modified from her original version. As you bring it into your prayer life, be patient with yourself. Remember that it is never easy to confront painful information, but that it strengthens our ability to do the work that is needed to cocreate with God a sustainable world.

. . . .

GUIDED MEDITATION: BREATHING THROUGH[2]

Closing your eyes, focus attention on your breathing. Don't try to breathe any special way, slow or long. Just watch the breathing as it happens, in and out. Note the accompanying sensations at the nostrils or upper lip, in the chest or abdomen. Let your mind rest there, focusing for now simply on the sensations of breathing. Stay passive and alert, like a cat by a mouse hole. (Pause).

Now visualize your breath as a stream or ribbon of air passing through you…see it flow up through your nose, down through your windpipe and into your lungs. Now from your lungs, take it through your heart. Picture it flowing through your heart and out through an opening there to reconnect with the larger family of creation. Let the breath-stream, as it passes through you, appear as one loop within that vast web of life, connecting you with it. (Pause.)

Now open your awareness to the suffering that is present in the world. Drop for now all defenses and open to your knowledge of that suffering. Let it come as concretely as you can—images of your fellow beings in pain and need, in fear and isolation, in prisons, hospitals, tenements, refugee camps. There is no need to strain for these images; they are present to you by virtue of our interexistence. Relax and just let them surface, the vast and countless hardships of our fellow humans, and of our animal brothers and sisters as well, as they swim the seas and fly through the air of this ailing planet. (Pause.) Now breathe in the pain like dark granules on the stream of air; up through your nose, down through your trachea, lungs and heart, and out again into the world net. You are asked to do nothing for now but let it pass through your heart. Be sure that the stream flows through and out again; don't hang onto the pain. Surrender it for now to the healing Spirit that breathes through all of life. (Pause.)

With Mother Teresa of Calcutta, we can say, "May God break my heart so completely that the whole world falls in."[3] When we let our own pain or the pain of others pass through our hearts, we create a space out of which a deep compassion for life can be borne. This type of breathing is similar to that of a woman in childbirth, bearing pain to bring forth life. As you breathe through this pain today, imagine joining with our Sister

Mother Earth, who "cries out in labor pains, longing for her fulfillment in God."

If no images or feelings arise and there is only blankness, greyness and numbness, breathe that through. The numbness itself is a very real part of our world. (Pause.) If what surfaces for you is not the pain of other beings so much as your own personal suffering, breathe that through, too. Your own anguish is an integral part of the grief of our world and arises with it.

Should you feel an ache in the chest, a pressure in the rib cage, as if the heart would break, that is all right. Your heart is not an object that can break. Our hearts cannot mourn for that which they do not love—it is a sign of your deep love and connection to the world. Hearts broken open create a fertile emptiness into which flow God's love and compassion for the world. Trust it. Keep breathing. (Pause.) As you take the time to be mindfully present to the pain in your own life, or the suffering of your sisters and brothers in the family of creation, remember that this kind of contemplative practice dilates your heart, "like a plant unfolding before Brother Sun's energy."

Remember again your kinship with God and all of creation and your desire to restore right relationship wherever you can. (Pause.) Make an intention to be mindful when you encounter pain today; instead of bracing against it, try to breathe it through, to let yourself be moved in compassion for your fellow beings, and start to notice what pain and suffering can teach you when you choose not to look away. Ask Francis and Clare for strength and courage to walk this contemplative path that is so necessary in today's world. Be open to the joy and freedom that comes with the courage of living a truly contemplative life. (Pause). And when you're ready, open your eyes.

• • • • • • • • • • • • • • • • • • •

"Francis, Go Rebuild My Oikos": Individual Actions

Another story from Francis' life shows us how his converted heart moved him to take the path of reflective action, despite difficulties he faced. Immediately after hearing the words, "Francis, go rebuild my house; as you see it is all being destroyed," Francis took action and began to rebuild the church, stone by stone. Yet after contemplating the situation further, he saw that God was calling him to transform the larger church of his time, spurring important reforms, which required him to confront some of the painful injustices happening then. If Francis were to sit in contemplative prayer today before the reality of our crucified Earth, might he not hear the same words within an even larger context? "Francis, go rebuild my *oikos*—my creation; as you see, it is all being destroyed." Rooted in a deep love for God's creation and the knowledge of God's interconnection with all created life, surely Francis would feel a spiritual mandate to act on its behalf—to protect and restore our God-given home. Yet so few Christians today make the connection between their practice of faith and this mandate to protect God's creation.

An important first step in contemplation involves taking an honest inventory of our behaviors and choices, assessing our own current level of impact on large-scale problems such as global climate change. This is necessary before we can make an effective plan to begin to restore right relationship in our lives, our communities and our world. This kind of assessment can also provide provocative material for individual and group reflection. In the spirit of Francis, we encourage you to view these suggested actions as more than a list of actions to check off one by one. Instead, let them become a spiritual practice that will help you *live into* a penitential lifestyle. Francis did not view penance as a duty or obligation, but as a way of life; living in harmony with God and creation brought him joy and gladness. A life of making amends to creation means restoring right relationship one action at a time, day after day, and discovering the joy and simplicity that flows from such a penitent life.

1. Calculate your carbon emissions. This quantifies how many pounds of carbon dioxide your household emits into the atmosphere annually, thus contributing directly to global climate change. This calculation can be achieved by completing the written carbon emissions assessment in Appendix C or by using one of the recommended Web-based carbon calculators listed there. You can use these measurements as a baseline for evaluating your progress—this concrete feedback can help not only inform your actions but also provide positive reinforcement as your "carbon footprint" begins to shrink. But many people ask, do individual choices really matter? In Portland, Oregon, the typical household generates 45,000 pounds of carbon dioxide annually—collectively 40 percent of the city's overall carbon dioxide emissions. Thus, our own individual lifestyle choices are a significant part of the problem, and the good news is that we as individuals can likewise be a significant part of the solution if we learn to make different choices.[4] The actions required to shrink our carbon emissions have far-reaching implications—they not only contribute significantly to curbing climate change, but also to saving habitats, slowing down the extinction of species and bringing global justice to poor countries in our world.

2. Become more conscious. The excesses of our levels of consumption in the United States stem partially from unconscious consumer habits and being unaware of the impacts of our choices. With just a little intention and not a lot of sacrifice, we can begin to shave off the excesses of the American footprint. Today start with eliminating any excesses you can—turn off your lights when not in use, don't leave the water running as you brush your teeth or wash your dishes. Limit your showers to five minutes, turn your heater down four degrees and your air conditioner up four degrees from your customary temperature. Recycle everything that you can in your area. Eat two more meat-free meals each week and combine errands to reduce trips in the car. Actions such as these begin to build our awareness of our impact and prepare us for taking the more significant actions discussed in chapter twelve.

3. Change your habits. The simple act of replacing one frequently used lightbulb with a compact fluorescent bulb can decrease your carbon dioxide emissions by 500 pounds a year. Leaving your car at home two days a week can keep almost 1,600 pounds of carbon dioxide from our atmosphere each year, and driving a car that gets thirty-two miles per gallon or better can annually save more than 5,600 pounds of carbon dioxide from being emitted.[5] Choose a good source and research further actions you can take to reduce your contributions to global climate change. (See Select Bibliography and Resources section for a listing of resources that provide actions to help you reduce your ecological and carbon footprint.)

Americans who have participated in citizen behavior change programs (aimed at ways they can reduce their carbon emissions) have collectively reduced their greenhouse gas emissions by over 100 million pounds in one decade.[6] Measure your impact (before and after) and give yourself credit for your effort!

4. Start small. Don't try to change too much at once. Many actions are listed in this chapter and chapter twelve, and some will come easier to you than others. Choose one that most connects to your heart, and approach it as a spiritual practice. Focus on it for a predetermined period of time (such as the Lenten season). Set small, attainable goals and build the new behavior into your life until it becomes second nature. And it is always helpful to remember Mother Teresa's advice: "We can do no great things, only small things with great love."

•

"FRANCIS, GO REBUILD MY OIKOS": GROUP REFLECTION
We have not yet learned how to adequately contemplate our environmental crisis. To do so, we would have to face difficult feelings such as grief, despair, anger, guilt and powerlessness. A necessary aspect of this contemplation, too, would be to examine all the ways our corporate-run, consumer society would have us look the other way and avoid the reality of what is happening to our world. Parker Palmer reminds us of

the countercultural nature of contemplation: "This is why the contemplative moment, the moment when illusion is stripped away and reality is revealed, is so hard to come by; there is a vast conspiracy against it."[7] Before we can begin to rebuild the *oikos,* we must take the time to fully contemplate the situation. We must take a step back and look at the situation with penetrating honesty. What prevents us from acting to protect God's creation?

The ecological devastation of our time is unprecedented, and the scale of the problems often feel insurmountable. Living in today's world, we are surrounded by bad news on all sides, and a quite natural human response is to look away and avoid the sobering truth. When we feel discouraged and powerless, apathy can take over so that, in the end, we shut down or do nothing. In fact, this "deadening of our response" [8] may be the biggest threat of all. How can it be that in today's world, when we have all the information necessary to tell us what's really happening, and the know-how we need to change, that we feel so immobilized and disempowered to act? What can we do to avoid shutting down to the overwhelming nature of these problems, so that we are available to be of service to creation?

Ecopsychologists believe that one of the reasons depression and anxiety have reached epidemic proportions in today's society is that many of us are responding to the collective heartache that is inevitable for conscious creatures whose habitat is being destroyed.[9] Just as a child cries for his mother when separated from her, we have become estranged from our Sister Mother Earth, on whom we are completely dependent for life. The mechanistic worldview of our society tells us that we are separate selves, and our fear, anger and despair must mean something is wrong with *us.* Our pain for the world, we are told, is rooted in our own personal problems rather than perhaps a normal, healthy response to the poisoning of our very life-support system. But a more holistic reframing of these feelings would be to understand them as a form of compassion for our world. These feelings may, in fact, be our planet's alarm signal—just what is needed for us to "wake up" and do what is required of us to change our ways.

If our pain is an inevitable response to what is going on around us, the pain is not the problem—but our repression of it is.[10] Modern-day society also sends powerful messages that discourage us from having or feeling such difficult emotions. The house of creation is crumbling all around us, yet if we begin to really contemplate this, discuss it or try to understand or act on this fact, we often hear messages such as:

How can you be such a doomsayer? Look at the bright side.
God will protect us—have a little faith!
Don't be such a downer, you'll fall apart or upset your family and friends.
I don't need to do anything—science and technology will save us from all this.

Feelings of despair, hopelessness and apathy are often the ones we welcome the least; we avoid these feelings for fear they will overwhelm us, depress others, make us look unpatriotic, unfaithful, weak or emotional. If we really look at the ways we ourselves contribute to the destruction of creation, we may experience tremendous guilt. We dislike feeling powerless or ignorant to such huge and complex issues as climate change or world hunger, so we avoid taking action. By consciously or unconsciously avoiding the issues, we avoid seeing reality as it truly is, and we are unable to act effectively.

Contemplation involves looking at all these internal barriers that keep us from engaging in our world and rebuilding the *oikos*. Yet it also includes examining the societal factors that influence the choices we make in our lives. Our actions will be ineffective or provide only temporary relief without an understanding of the underlying forces which cause us to act unconsciously to harm our own habitat—our home. In today's society consumerism exerts an ever-increasing impact on our choices. These forces are so pervasive that it is difficult to be aware of all the ways they influence us. Brian Swimme warns that our media and consumeristic culture now exert a bigger influence on our children than our churches: "The fact that consumerism has become the dominant world-faith is largely invisible to us, so it is helpful to understand clearly that to hand our children over to the consumer culture is to place them in the care of the planet's most sophisticated religious preachers."[11] Ours is a fast-paced, instant gratification culture that would have us stay on the surface and avoid looking at the harder, deeper questions. The depth of reflection and interiority that is required of true contemplation is made difficult in the midst of these powerful cultural forces. This is where our Christian faith comes in.

What would it mean for us Christians to truly take a contemplative stance on an ailing planet? The following activity is designed for a group, but the questions can also be used individually for reflection.[12] It is designed to help us look at the situation of global climate change with seeing eyes, to become aware of our own ways of coping with or avoiding difficult feelings associated with the bad news of our world, and to examine the individual, social and societal influences that contribute to our inept collective human response to our most pressing ecological crises. The structure of the activity allows us to express our pain for the world, and for our part in its destruction, without fear of being censored or judged, as well as to simply listen, with no need to respond.

As preparation for this activity it is recommended that each group member measure his or her own carbon footprint beforehand (see activity earlier in this chapter). When the group convenes, divide the members into pairs and have them sit facing each other, far enough from other pairs that they can hear their partners talk. Have the pairs determine who will be Partner A and Partner B. When the guide speaks each unfinished sentence, A will then repeat it and complete it in his or her own words, continuing to talk as spontaneously as possible until the guide rings a bell (one to two minutes later), indicating it is time to finish. If Partner A runs out of things to say, he or she can simply return to the sentence again, as many times as needed. (While explaining this exercise, it is very important to note that Partner B should listen *silently* as Partner A speaks.) Their only focus is to listen as receptively and supportively as possible. When Partner A has finished, the guide repeats the same question, and Partner B answers for the same amount of time, with Partner A listening in silence. After both partners have answered, and before moving onto the next question, allow for a few moments of silence, emphasizing breathing and nonverbal appreciation for each others' sharing. Depending on the time you have, choose anywhere from three to five of the questions below or create your own to fit your specific group and situation.

- When I look at the ways that we humans are destroying God's creation through global climate change, what concerns me most is…
- Common responses to a reality as large-scale as global climate change are: denial, fear, anger, despair. Feelings I have had when I have heard about climate change are…
- When I contemplate the reality of global climate change, some of the ways I avoid the difficult feelings that arise are…
- I am sometimes reluctant to share these feelings and responses with loved ones because…
- Ways these feelings and responses could be useful to me if I chose to face rather than hide from them are…
- Imagine God spoke to you, like Francis, saying, "Go, rebuild my *oikos*, my creation, for it is being destroyed." For me, in these times, God would be calling me to…
- Some things I am willing to do in order to reduce my own carbon dioxide emissions are…
- Some things I may have to give up in order to do this, and begin to live in right relationship with creation are…
- When I think about making these changes, I feel…
- What I look forward to about making these changes is…

When the pairs have finished the chosen questions, gather into a large group to allow participants to express anything about the experience that they would like to share. When doing despair work, such as in this activity, it is important to give people adequate time to move through the emotional process required. Usually participants feel more empowered after completing the entire activity, simply because they have been able to express difficult feelings in an accepting atmosphere. As a facilitator of this type of process, it is important to be prepared to help the group honor and hold difficult feelings being voiced or experienced, and to guide the process through its natural course.[13] As a guide, it is your duty to "hold the container" for the painful feelings being expressed, and to redirect anyone who is trying to problem-solve or offer a "quick fix." It is also helpful to use periods of silence, and to have a reading or a song prepared with which to end. The following is an excellent prayer to bring a session like this to a close:

> Oh, God of all, at this time of our gradual awakening
> to the dangers we are imposing on our beautiful Earth,
> open the hearts and minds of all your children,
> that we may learn to nurture rather than destroy our planet.
> Amen.[14]

Of course, after an individual or group has spent time with the above questions, it is also important to discern how best to join with God to "rebuild the *oikos*" and take action to heal our world! The reflective action suggestions in chapter twelve will offer several concrete ideas for how to begin this important step in an engaged Franciscan spirituality.

NOTES

[1] Parker J. Palmer, *The Active Life: A Spirituality of Work, Creativity, and Caring* (New York: Jossey-Bass, 1990), p. 17.

[2] Joanna Macy, *Coming Back to Life: Practices to Reconnect Our Lives, Our World* (Gabriola Island, B.C.: New Society, 1998), pp. 190–191.

[3] David James Duncan, "What Fundamentalists Need For Their Salvation," *Orion Online,* July/August 2005 available from http://www.oriononline.org.

[4] Global Action Plan for the Earth, *Low Carb Diet/Cool Portland Campaign* (New York: Global Action Plan for the Earth, 2001), p. 1.

[5] *Climate Solutions: Practical Solutions to Global Warming,* "15 Top Things You Can Do To Reduce Global Warming," available from www.climatesolutions.org.

[6] *Low Carb Diet/Cool Portland Campaign,* p. 2. An updated version of this program, *Low Carbon Diet Climate Change Program: A 30-Day Program to Lose 5000 Pounds* (by David Gershon) can now be purchased through Empowerment Institute, http://www.empowermentinstitute.net.

[7] Palmer, p. 26.

[8] Macy, p. 24.

[9] These insights are gleaned from several sources, including Macy, p. 49; Theodore Roszak, *The Voice of the Earth: An Exploration of Ecopsychology* (Grand Rapids: Phanes, 2001), pp. 320–321; Liz Galst, "Global Worrying: The Environment Is in Peril and Anxiety Disorders Are on the Rise. What's the Connection?" *Plenty* (August/September 2006), p. 55.

[10] I am indebted to Joanna Macy for the concepts in this section, which draws heavily on her writings about grief and despair due to our ecological crises. For a more detailed summary, see "The Greatest Danger: Apatheia, The Deadening of Mind and Heart," in *Coming Back to Life,* pp. 25–38.

[11] Brian Swimme, *Hidden Heart of the Cosmos: Humanity and the New Story* (Maryknoll, N.Y.: Orbis, 1996), p. 14.

[12] This activity is adapted from the "Open Sentences" activity in Macy, pp. 98–100.

[13] For helpful tips handling strong emotions while leading group activities such as this, refer to "Guiding Group Work," chapter five, in Macy, pp. 63–80, or *The Work That Reconnects* (training DVD), available from New Society, 2007.

[14] Lorraine R. Schmitz, "A Prayer For Peace," *Eco-Ministry News: Interfaith Network for Earth Concerns,* Ecumenical Ministries of Oregon, Spring 2003, p. 4.

·

·

·

·

·

part four

CREATION
AND
CONVERSION

chapter ten

THE ECOLOGY OF CONVERSION

Human beings are the cause of our planet's environmental crises. We have no one else to blame. We are all responsible to some degree in this unfolding tragedy, and we are all bearing some of the negative effects. The biodiversity crisis and global climate change threaten the integrity of God's creation, but pollution of all kinds threatens the bodily integrity and medical health of everyone. This chapter will lay out elements of a vision for transforming the relationship between humans and the rest of creation, inspired by the conversion of Saint Francis. The poor man of Assisi was the most celebrated saint of the Middle Ages because he spoke to his contemporary society of God, his life spoke of the possibility of living out the good news. In the face of rising violence and greed in his society, Francis' life testified to alternatives of peace and simplicity. His practice of poverty, humility and contemplative prayer can help us change the direction of our society. Francis preached conversion of heart, to individuals and to groups, and this strategy is needed more than ever today. Ultimately, to progress toward a more sustainable world, we will have to embody the values of compassion, wisdom and integrity, both as individuals and as communities.

•

OUR ENVIRONMENTAL CRISES

Transformation, like conversion, is an appealing yet threatening term. We know that we cannot continue to treat the Earth with such disregard, with such abuse. All but the most disingenuous Americans recognize that future generations will inherit a planet that is more polluted, biologically impoverished and climatically unstable relative to the one we received. We know that we humans have made some foolish choices. As a whole, America has become the most affluent country in the history of human civilization, but the environmental costs of this affluence have been tremendous. Our desire for consumer goods reaches across the globe to gobble up natural resources, and our energy systems consume massive amounts of fossil fuel. Americans produce more than twice as much carbon dioxide per person as Europeans or Japanese people,[1] yet the United States federal government has been the greatest obstacle to addressing global climate change. The sheer number of humans impacts the health of ecosystems and biological diversity, but the greatest threat is posed by our high-consumption, American lifestyle. Resource consumption multiplies the impact of every person. For example, every American child will consume more energy in his or her lifetime than fifty Indian children.

These are but a few troubling aspects to our environmental crises. Many have written about specific acts that individuals can do to reduce their environmental impact, some of which can be found in the bibliography. A great deal of information about these practices is widely available in newspapers and on Web sites. What we lack today is a profound desire for change, for transforming our relationship with our home planet, and to understand how to pursue this. Here again, Francis provides a model.[2] His conversion began with taking personal responsibility for himself and his actions, but he then reached out to others to engage them in collective social transformation. He undertook concrete initiatives to persuade others to change their behavior, and this inspired later theologians to frame these initiatives as manifesting justice. Today understanding our ecological footprint and working toward a more sustainable society can carry forward this Franciscan vision of conversion.

The ecological footprint can further our conversion by helping us to perceive the impact of our choices, as individuals, households, communities and nations. From one perspective it is merely an accounting tool, tracking the resources we consume and waste and we throw "away." By measuring everything that comes into our personal *oikos*—whether individual households, or community, or state or nation—we can assess the amount of land (and sea) from which we draw resources, whether for food, fiber, water or energy. The Earth can only generate a limited amount of plant and animal products, also known as biological productivity. Finite amounts of fossil fuel are buried in the earth, and only so much rain and snow fall from the sky each year. Recognizing the impact we have on the Earth by dumping our waste—trash, sewage, toxic or carbon dioxide pollution—can also stimulate a desire to simplify our lives. Many organizations make the ecological footprint tool available for individuals to assess their own environmental impact. Some cities, states and nations have used it to measure their consumption and to develop an agenda for change: targeted goals for reducing their impact. Harvard biologist Edward O. Wilson regards the ecological footprint as one of the most important contemporary applications of ecology because it allows ordinary people to recognize the environmental implications of their behavior. This tool helps us to see the implications of our consumption choices and to compare the impact of different choices, by individuals and social groups.

•

GRIM REALITY

Here's the grim news: Due to our high-consumption lifestyle, the average American has an annual footprint of twenty-four acres, the greatest per-person impact in the world. It would take five "Earths" full of resources to supply the entire human family with an American lifestyle. For reference, the global average is about seven acres per person, but even that level of consumption cannot be maintained indefinitely. It takes about fifteen months of biological productivity to support the annual global average of consumption. Simply put, we humans are living beyond our ecological means, what the *oikos* can support. Another way to use the footprint is calculate the size of human population that could be maintained in a United States lifestyle. Working backward, roughly 1.2 billion people could be sustained at our standard of living, but of course, we share the planet with more than six billion other humans.[3] Reducing our consumption is simultaneously an ecological and social justice issue.

If everyone in the world consumed as much as Americans do, we would need four additional planets full of resources to supply us. But of course, there are no other planets to support these consumptive habits. God made the *oikos* finite, and from contemplation of the Incarnation, we can conclude that God is pleased with a finite creation. The fate of humans and that of the rest of creation are the same. The problem is human sinfulness, human greed. We humans are taking more than our share of the Earth's goods, and throwing away too much "waste." So what happens ecologically when a population—people or other creatures—consumes more resources than the Earth can produce? Ecologists term this situation "overshoot." When humans—households, states or nations—demand more than the biological productivity their local area can provide—also known as carrying capacity—they impact other people, places and future generations. They also impact the health of ecosystems. Figure 3 illustrates the problem of overshoot. As consumption levels continue to rise, it crosses the threshold of the biological carrying capacity. That intersection marks the upper limit of sustainable consumption. Above that carrying capacity, the demand for additional resources must be met by cutting into the ability of ecosystems to produce in the future or by drawing resources from some other region.

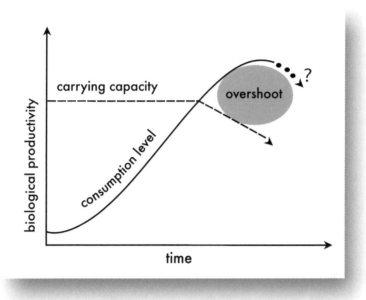

Figure 3. Overshoot.

An analogy from accounting helps illustrate this. Imagine you have a bank account of $100.00, and it earns 5 percent interest. So long as you do not withdraw more than $5.00 per year, you can continue to live off the interest. If you decide you need $10.00 or $20.00 each year, you can withdraw more for a while—thus diminishing your interest payments in the future—or you can take resources from someone else. Of the twenty-four acres per person required to support the consumption patterns of an average American, ten acres on average of resources are drawn from other countries.[4] Consuming resources beyond the Earth's capacity to regenerate them is a form of stealing from future generations or other places. Overshoot can continue for a period of time, but in nature eventually a population outstrips its ability to support itself with resources, and the population contracts dramatically. Humans have used technology to cope with some of these resource limitations, and demonstrated remarkable creativity, but resource demands—oil, water, fertile soil, energy—are outpacing the technological creativity. And the urgency for the resources has brought with it not only ecological problems, but socioeconomic and political ones as well and in many cases has provoked wars and mass-human tragedy, as humans battle for what little is left.

•

OUR FAIR "EARTHSHARE"

To live justly in relationship to other beings on the planet, Americans need to live within our "fair earthshare." This is calculated by taking all of the ecologically productive land on the Earth and dividing it by the total world population. This works out to about five acres per person, which would be about 20 percent of the average American consumption level.[5] At what point can we begin to name our American addiction to consumption as greed? Our consumption patterns are an injustice to the Earth and to the poor. Why is it so difficult for Americans to talk about greed? This truly is our cultural blind spot. We have blessed greed and called it a virtue! This points us to the justice dimension of sustainability. The concept of sustainability offers a vision for a more just and environmentally responsible society. Making progress toward sustainability requires addressing relationships between humans as well as between humans and the environment, as Figure 4 illustrates. Some people have used the concept in merely a scientific, technical sense, but this is a mistake, because we cannot progress toward a more sustainable society without addressing questions of economic development and social justice. The schema in Figure 4 has also been called an e-3 diagram, referring to ecology, economics and equity. A genuine vision of sustainability necessarily requires an integration of all three.

Figure 4. Sustainability's Venn diagram

With one billion people living on one dollar a day, and another billion living on but two, additional economic development in the global South is a moral imperative. This one-third of the human family needs to increase its consumption so that they can live with greater dignity, and these countries cannot do so without initiatives for justice from the politically powerful industrial nations. The global economic system—trade, banking, industry—must be reformed so as to facilitate economic development for these very poor people. But this will require reducing American consumption, and this is where questions of equity come to the fore. We must find a way to reduce our consumption, reduce our ecological footprint, not only for the sake of the Earth but also for the sake of the very poor. We Americans have a special responsibility to turn away from our affluence and embrace the practice of humility and simplicity. This does not mean we will return to living in caves by candlelight! The average citizen of the United Kingdom lives quite comfortably yet has an ecological footprint half the size of a person living in the United States. This fact alone raises troubling questions about the greed and wastefulness of American society. The United Kingdom has made different economic choices than the United States has, and that country impacts the Earth on average much less than we do.

•

HOW DO WE REDUCE CONSUMPTION?

Reducing American consumption levels is the most important environmental task before us. It will require greater ecological understanding of creation, but that alone will not be enough. It will require changing economic structures, but that will prove very difficult without popular support. At its core, the transition to a sustainable society will require conversion of individual hearts as well as social institutions. Initiatives by individuals and households are very important because they orient our lives toward this goal. But individual actions alone will not suffice. We must find a way to engage the economic and political institutions that structure our consumption patterns. Ultimately, the individual and the social are intertwined because our individual choices as Americans are largely determined by the options available to us in our society. For example, individuals can do a great deal to conserve energy in their homes by moderating their heating in the winter and air conditioning in the summer. Economic studies have shown that the greatest energy (and economic) savings can be found in more efficient buildings. Homes can be remodeled, but this can be expensive, costing more in the short term. It may take years to result in savings. The most effective way to reduce household energy consumption is to require new structures to be highly energy efficient, but this requires forethought in design and public support for building codes. In another example, public transportation uses much less fossil fuel per mile traveled relative to other forms of transportation, but many areas of the country—including some cities—

have not made this a viable option. Other industrialized countries have invested in public transportation, and they make it work rather well, conserving fossil energy and improving the quality of people's lives.

•

REVOLUTION AS CONVERSION

Revolution is another word for conversion. Francis led a revolution of love, peace and compassion in his day. A contemporary Franciscan response to our ecological crises should be participation in the sustainability revolution, a movement in human society no less dramatic in scale than the Industrial Revolution.[6] William McDonough and Michael Braungart refer to this as the next Industrial Revolution.[7] This conversion, this turning, is already underway. In fact, many businesses are leading this effort, as they recognize that we are entering a new era of environmental uncertainty, and that reducing energy use and pollution through wise design is good for the bottom line as well as the planet. McDonough and Braungart argue that human society must redesign its economy informed by ecological knowledge, proposing three simple but revolutionary principles. First, waste equals food. In nature, there is no such thing as waste. Every packet of energy, every scrap of nutrition is put to use by some creature. They argue that achieving sustainability will require us to eliminate the very concept of waste, for it does not exist in nature. Everything that is left over, whether energy or waste materials, can be incorporated into sustainable industrial processes. Second, use available solar energy. Every step toward reducing fossil fuel use and increasing solar energy use is a step toward sustainability. This can be as simple as an individual hanging up clothes to dry in the sun instead of using an electric dryer, or as sophisticated as an urban area investing in a public transportation system. Third, value biological diversity. Nature is woven together by diversity, and all life depends upon the function and structure of diversity in ecosystems. One way to do this is to adjust one's diet to local seasonal foods, thus supporting smaller farmers and regional food distribution systems. These three "simple" principles can be applied widely, to almost any kind of system: buildings, transportation, agriculture and food and industry. They cannot be applied simply, however, for they require us to redesign our systems, indeed, many systems of systems, including our economy. The sustainability revolution requires a transformation of society and also how we think about our bodies in relationship to other humans and the rest of creation. The most dramatic progress will take place as political and economic institutions undergo conversion, but that will not happen without a transformation of consciousness, and this points to the special role that Franciscan spirituality can play. We have to take individual responsibility for our own lives and households, but that alone is not enough. We must call others to repentance as well, individuals and institutions, to live more simply.

The sustainability revolution must address our relationship with technology, for our misuse of technology has been a major cause of environmental degradation. Many people think of technology as a universal panacea, a solution to every problem, but this is misplaced faith. As a society we are not likely to recognize the problems associated with our technologies unless we begin to understand them in an ecological framework. We have to think about the impact that raw material extraction and manufacturing have, plus the impact of their ultimate disposal (as Figure 1 on page 32 illustrated). During the 1990s this approach to industrial ecology was called "cradle to grave," but the sustainability revolution has challenged those designing technologies to think in terms of "cradle to cradle," meaning all the components should be able to be reused, recycled or composted. We need technologies for the sustainability revolution, for example renewable energy production and more efficient forms of transportation, but even more than new technologies, we have to develop critical thinking skills to evaluate what kind of technologies can promote human dignity, social justice and sustainability.

This call to simplify our collective lifestyles, to act in greater solidarity with the poorest members of the human family, to undergo transformation of consciousness and values, is fully consistent with the

Franciscan tradition. Francis did not merely announce good news, but he and the early Franciscans undertook concrete initiatives to bring about peace between warring parties. Francis wrote letters to lay Franciscans, to leaders of the early friars, to clergy and to "the rulers of the peoples." Most of these writings addressed church reforms after the Fourth Lateran Council, but they also contained a call to public repentance, to a change of heart and social values as well. Francis and the early Franciscans engaged the pressing social and political questions of their day, bringing a gospel perspective to them. Francis addressed those who followed his example, whether vowed or secular, but also the political leaders of his era. He was the herald of the Great King, and understood this as calling all creatures back to a relationship of reverence, respect and humility with our Creator. Being a herald of the Great King today means calling others to live in right relationship with Creator and creation.

Conversion in the Franciscan tradition always has a public dimension. Repentance must begin in the human heart, but its transformative implications radiate outward into society and the world. Francis described himself as a penitent, dedicating himself to the practice of compassion and the preaching of justice. Sustainability offers contemporary followers of Francis a conceptual framework for restoring right relationship—with each other and the Earth. Building on this tradition is our challenge today, for those of us who wish to follow the patron saint of ecology. We are called to simplify our lifestyles, to find ways of living that reflect our belief in the goodness and integrity of creation, but that alone is not sufficient. We, too, must find ways of engaging other members of our society and dominant social values, and call them to conversion of heart and life. Developing and articulating such a transformative vision is the fundamental task for the Franciscan movement in the twenty-first century.

NOTES

[1] Gore, *An Inconvenient Truth*.

[2] Leonardo Boff, *St. Francis: A Model of Human Liberation* (New York: Crossroad, 1982).

[3] Christopher Uhl, *Developing Ecological Consciousness* (Lanham, Md.: Rowman and Littlefield, 2004), pp. 175–179.

[4] Uhl, pp. 77–79.

[5] For discussion, see Mathis Wackernagel and William Rees, *Our Ecological Footprint: Reducing Human Impact on the Earth* (Philadelphia: New Society Publishers, 1996).

[6] Andres R. Edwards, *The Sustainability Revolution: Portrait of a Paradigm Shift* (Gabriola Island, B.C.: New Society, 2005).

[7] See the video *The Next Industrial Revolution*. See also Uhl, pp. 264–266.

chapter eleven

THE SPIRITUALITY OF CONVERSION

We find ourselves today in a perilous situation with regard to the environment. If the universe is likened to a hospital, planet Earth is in critical condition in the intensive care unit. The critical state of the environmental situation is so outside our daily experience of life, however, that it is as if we humans are lounging at the snack bar while Earth struggles to breathe. We could wait until disaster really strikes before we attend to Earth's dying needs. However, as Christians, waiting for disaster to strike the Earth that feeds us contradicts our hope for a new heaven and a new Earth. We are called to love God *in* creation, not apart from creation. Incarnation means that creation is the co-beloved of God, not a commodity for human consumption. God loves creation so much that God has entered into it in a personal way. To participate in the family of creation is the most fundamental Christian stance for those who claim to believe in the Body of Christ.

•

CHRISTIAN UNCONSCIOUSNESS

We live, however, with a dichotomy of beliefs—a type of "Christian unconsciousness." We pray to God as creator of heaven and Earth, yet we relate to God as if God might have little to do with Earth. How do we offer gifts of bread and wine each week at Sunday Mass and destroy wheat fields to build factories to manufacture cars whose parts are made in another part of the world where the average salary is two dollars a day? How do we consume copious amounts of water and not care about the scarcity of this resource in parts of the world where people are dying of thirst—literally? How can we drive cars to go food shopping two miles away when many people around the world walk or use public transportation? We live indeed with a type of "functional unconsciousness." We celebrate the goodness of creation made holy by the Incarnation and we pollute or destroy that same creation by unconscious acts of self-centeredness. We are in a very serious condition.

Kenan Osborne highlights two central characteristics of our contemporary society that impact our relationship to Earth: First, our obsession with technology and science, and second, our antireligious secularism. Both of these characteristics support a defense of human autonomy shown as an exercise of freedom independent from God. As a result, contemporary society is rationally fragmented; our ability to live a fully human life is endangered.[1] Through consumerism and technological advance we have increasingly turned the human person and the goods of the Earth into commodities—"its"—for personal or exploitive use. And sadly, we have lost sight of the power of greed because the World Wide Web has lured us into "virtual Christianity." Pressing a button that charges five dollars to our credit card to feed a child in Africa is our "feel good" sense of Christian community. Although the computer may be helpful for data access or writing papers, it may also be robbing us of our divine vocation or at least making us think that divinization can come about through e-mail. Technology may enhance the quality of life, but it may also suppress the mystical dimension of life by providing instant gratification and immediate, visible results. As a result, we no longer know how to stand patiently between God's indwelling and God's transcendence. We have become blind to the "burning bush" experience of God, so blind, in fact, that we burn the bush ourselves in order to build a shopping mall. We are destroying modes of God's self-revelation bit by bit.

The life of Francis of Assisi holds an essential lesson for us, a fundamental attitude that needs to be recovered today, if Earth is to live into a healthy future. That attitude is conversion. From the beginning of his life Francis was led to "do penance." The word *penance* comes from the Greek *metanoia*. In ancient Greece, *metanoia* meant "the shifting of minds" and referred to the way one arrived at a new way of looking at a situation or a new understanding of an issue. The word *conversion* conveys a similar meaning of "turning." Conversion is not something we "do" as an action. One does not perform acts of repentance; rather, one repents or, we might say, one is in repentance. Conversion is a way of becoming more authentically human—through turning. Doing penance as a way of life led Francis to a series of conversions or "turnings" early on in his spiritual life: from a life of luxury and frivolity to the service of lepers, from the life of the merchant to the life of the hermit in solitude and from the life of the hermit to the life of preaching the gospel. That is why penance governed Francis' entire life because it is what he did throughout his life, continuously turning from the gravity of sin and self-centeredness toward the gravity of God. There is no doubt that this turning was not entirely a human effort, something apart from God's grace. Rather, Francis discovered that grace, freely given, is the energy of "turning" as one single movement with God. To be receptive to grace is to acknowledge that one is a creature of God. Francis came to realize that everything in his life was gift because his life was grace-filled.

As we hover on the brink of global destruction, conversion may be the grace that saves us from destroying the Earth and ourselves in the process. If conversion is a grace-filled movement, it is also the grace of "unlearning" because it takes real effort to undo what is learned behavior so that we may learn anew for the sake of the future. Scientists today are discovering that certain areas of the brain are involved in religion and that prayer may entail certain neural patterns. The human brain is "wired for God." Sin, we might say, is a "short circuit" in this wiring process. It is the unraveling of the God-centered pattern that causes us to act in harmful ways. We can describe conversion, therefore, as "rewiring" the brain. It is redirecting unhealthy patterns of behavior toward new patterns that are more life-giving. This rewiring process of conversion is a movement away from the past and toward the future because the present and the past are antagonistic, while the present and the future are immutably one. To turn away from patterns of behavior that isolate us from one another or from the earth is to face our prejudices and hidden biases that create fear, mistrust and suspicion of another. Through a life of conversion Francis of Assisi was "rewired" for God.

The story of the wolf of Gubbio is a good example of Francis' life of conversion. In the small town of Gubbio a ferocious wolf was terrorizing the people. When Francis came to visit, they told him of the wolf and their fears of attack. Francis confronted the wolf, as a mother would her child, and reprimanded the wolf for causing such turmoil in the town. But Francis also realized that the wolf was terrorizing the people out of extreme hunger. The wolf had needs but the people were too frightened to even take notice of his needs. Francis, however, drew close to the wolf, made the Sign of the Cross on him and spoke to him, commanding him not to harm anyone. The wolf submitted to Francis' plea for peace and, in turn, Francis promised the wolf food for the rest of his days, as long as the wolf agreed not to harm anyone. From then on, the wolf became a friend of the people and a peaceful companion in the little town of Gubbio.[2] Why is this story a story of conversion? Because it tells us that when we are turned toward God, we can confront the needs of creation as they are presented to us and respond to them not out of fear or self-defense but out of a heart full of mercy and love. Only when we live in the attitude of "turning toward God" do we overcome fear and attitudes that isolate us from one another or from nonhuman creatures.

In her book *Releasement*, Barbara Fiand describes an attitude of "letting be." The term *releasement* means letting things be themselves without trying to impose another form on them. Conversion is a type of releasement because it is a movement toward "letting be."[3] It is allowing the other to be other without placing excessive demands on it or trying to manipulate it to one's own liking or advantage. This requires a turning toward the other in such a way that one's attention is away from self-concern and self-preoccupation and turned to the other as the basis of self. But to turn away from self toward the other requires that one be at home with oneself, allowing oneself to be. Conversion, therefore, is not simply turning toward the other as a denial of self but turning to the other as an acceptance of self; indeed, as part of oneself. When we do not allow ourselves "to be" we do not allow others "to be" either. We can become impatient with our own infirmities and finitude just as we become impatient with others. Conversion is the maturity of accepting interdependence as the definition of life and of life in the universe. The person who lives in the spirit of conversion can embrace others as they are without trying to forge them into something they are not.

Francis allowed others to be themselves, and in this "letting be" he saw God. He saw that flowers standing by the side of the road gazing into the face of God were holy because they did what they were created to do, give God praise and glory. Poor persons and lepers were icons of Christ because they could not be anything other than themselves. Rocks and water, bees and trees all did what they were created to do, and Francis recognized this "do-being" as the glory of God. Francis' life of penance or conversion was a lifelong turning to the unfolding beauty of God's love in creation. He realized that creation is nothing in itself because its being is a constant flow outward from God, whose nature is giving. Fiand writes:

> This flow outward receives its affirmation in our virgin mothering because we are released toward it. We can embrace things; we can let them be. We are opened up to wonder, from the prison of determination and opened to mystery. Things no longer possess us. We stand near them but not in them.[4]

In a sense, letting things "be" defines conversion because it is a turning away from control and manipulation and turning toward the other as the revelation of God. This "letting be" complements what Scotus means by justice, which is giving someone or something what it deserves. For Scotus, God's love and generosity merits a similar response by us humans, loving things as they are because of their inherent goodness. No act of choice can take place in the absence of an object or something to be chosen since the moral act is an act of the intellect, and the proper act of the intellect, according to Scotus, is love.[5] To be rational is not to be abstractly intellectual; rather, it is to love well. Francis was able to love the creatures of Earth not merely as objects to be interpreted, but as symbols, real expressions of God's life poured out in abundance on Earth. By allowing things to be, Francis discovered the awesome mystery of God's goodness in the simple ordinariness of being. In this way, everything became a gift to Francis, and in receiving the many gifts of God in creation, Francis went about with a heart full of gratitude and love. In accepting the goodness of others and the things of creation, Francis accepted himself as part of creation. In giving to others the gift of being, he was gifted in his own being. Thus, in creative openness he articulated his oneness with God.

•

CONVERSION TOWARD THE EARTH

The life of Francis shows us that, because of Jesus Christ, conversion toward the human person is conversion toward the Earth. As his life deepened in Christ, so too did it deepen in relation to others and the Earth itself. Through the lens of his life we see that we cannot turn toward the Earth and its creatures if we cannot turn toward the neighbor or stranger. We cannot advocate animal rights if we cannot advocate the rights of the poor. How do we come to dwell in this spirit of conversion? How can conversion become a way of life and not another goal to attain? We see in the life of Francis that conversion requires discipline or asceticism. We need practices that will help us "rewire" our attitudes and behaviors toward a God-centered life. Francis treated his body harshly throughout his life by fasting from food and sleep, by eating unsavory food sprinkled with ashes, sometimes eating leftover scraps or whatever was available. He dressed in shabby clothes, often giving his tunic away to others who seemed in greater need or refusing the warmth of woolen clothes, despite the bitter winter cold. This type of asceticism is unhealthy, yet there is a romantic appeal about it. To deny oneself food or clothes or the warmth of material comforts for the love of Christ tells us something about the human person. We are made for God and sometimes will undergo radical measures in order to find God or to make God present to us. The desire to renounce material things indicates that material things can suffocate out life-giving values such as love, care, concern and God-centeredness, if they are not held in balance. James Nash describes a virtue of "frugality" for our times. Such a virtue "denotes moderation, temperance, thrift, cost-effectiveness, efficient usage, and a satisfaction with material sufficiency."[6] It is the virtue of "enough-ness" that does not hoard or appropriate excess goods at the expense of another. It is living in the spirit of moderation, realizing that happiness does not come with a gift coupon but with a heart centered in God.

•

FROM HOMO SAPIENS TO HOMO OECONOMICUS

In her book *Life Abundant* Sally McFague describes opposition to frugality with the emergence of *Homo oeconomicus*, the consumer who lives amid material splendor and the producer who bends the Earth to virtually unrestrained human purpose.[7] The difference between the consumer and the frugal person is that the frugal person uses what he or she needs, whereas the consumer needs more than one can use and thus consumes. The transition of the average American today into *Homo oeconomicus* is alarming. As one former student wrote, consumerism has subverted our identity as human beings. Rationalism is no longer the basis of the human subject, now it is consumerism: "I buy, therefore, I am." Consumerism is the number-one killer of our time, snuffing out families, marriages and friendships, as well as brotherhood and sisterhood in creation. Loaded down by inanimate objects, such as computers, cars, televisions, clothes and whatever else we accumulate, we cannot step outside the crammed rooms of our lives. Life is like a station wagon on an open highway, filled to the brim with suitcases, beach equipment, chairs and piles of clothes. One wonders how the driver can see to change lanes since the back window is blocked by an inordinate amount of things piled high to the ceiling. Since even changing lanes is obscured by things, the driver stays in the same lane, coasting along, unconcerned about the length of traffic accumulating in the rear. We are on our own private journeys, and we don't really care who is behind us.

One of the perils of consumerism (and there are many) is a deadening of the senses to the human person and things of creation. Blinded by material things and addicted to consumption, we fail to see each person and creature as unrepeatable, unique creations of God, beings of inherent goodness worthy of our utmost attention. Conversion of the *Homo oeconomicus* means raising the deadened senses to life and opening their portals to others. The "unlearning" and turning of conversion involves recognition of our fundamental relatedness to the whole, not just other people but the earth itself. Unless we can find ourselves in solidarity with, rather than in control of (or indifferent to) the whole, we risk global disaster. Christian responsibility, especially for the natural world, demands that we think of the earth, and the entire cosmos for that matter, as our *home*—the place of our family. We must attempt to shift from a metaphysics of consumerism to a metaphysics of love, from mechanistic consumption to life-giving relationships whereby others, including nature, are active partners in the pursuit of God.

•

A New Turn to the Earth

In her 1996 presidential address to the Catholic Theological Society of America, Elizabeth Johnson claimed that the whole cosmos is the astonishing image of God. What we need, she indicated, is a new "turn to the Earth," an ability to rethink and refeel our connectedness to nature as a whole. If Francis learned to feel solidarity with creation through a deep, prayerful relationship with Christ, what do *we* need to feel part of the whole? How can we regain a sense of mystery in our lives where we truly live in the midst of God's indwelling presence and God's transcendence, where creation is recognized as the revelation of God's gracious goodness, and where the inherent dignity of each living being is recognized and valued as expressing the infinite love of God? We need, as Richard Gaillardetz points out, a new asceticism to accompany an ecological spirituality that incorporates the web of life in religious expression. On a practical note, we need to make wise choices when choices are presented to us. Can we use technology to promote a Franciscan vision of society? To promote social justice and the sustainability revolution? Can we use technology to serve the common good, or are we addicted to using it in gratifying our individualistic consumer desires? How can we together develop the wisdom to use technology appropriately? Asceticism or the practice of personal discipline for the sake of spiritual order is necessary to restore a balanced relationship to the Earth.

One does wonder if the prejudice against the Incarnation that Chinnici describes is indeed at the core of our unconsciously selfish behavior. If we really *do not* believe that God dwells in humanity and in creation, if that which exists does not have life-giving value but is brute matter, then it is reasonable that the selfish subject seeks his or her identity at the expense of others. We can then truly measure ourselves by the GNP: Greed, Nobody but me and Power. Even the Eucharist becomes another type of consumption for the *Homo oeconomicus,* taking in for oneself without sharing what one has received. Conversion to the Earth means turning from oneself as an individual, self-consuming subject toward an ecological self, a self interwoven in the web of life, dependent on others and on the things of this Earth. The ecological self, shaped by its relatedness to others, requires a feeling of belonging to others, including nature. Prayer is that life-giving relationship with God that opens the eyes of the human heart to the truth of the world immersed in the goodness of God. Francis spent long hours in prayer, often in wooded places or deserted caves. Through prayer he came to know himself as a humble creature of God. Prayer enabled him to see things for what they are in their individual creation, each uniquely loved into being by a God of infinite love.

To stand in creation, in openness to God's goodness, requires a prayerful, penetrating vision. Only in this way do we recognize that the other is where we encounter God and the truth of ourselves in God. It means putting aside our busyness and turning our attention to God and thus to others in whom God dwells. Because prayer is relationship with God, it means nurturing this relationship through a heartfelt awareness of God's presence. But this type of prayerful, penetrating vision requires time to deepen. The modern mind-set cannot comprehend that "dead time" of which modern technology tries to rid us is often the arena of grace. In her Madeleva Lecture, Kathleen Norris observed that "it always seems that just when daily life seems most unbearable...that what is inmost breaks forth, and I realize that what had seemed 'dead time' was actually a period of gestation."[8] In our feverish obsession to fill our lives with more things that give us what we want, instantly, without effort or engagement, we seem to cut ourselves off from the grace dimensions of life and from attentiveness to the humility of God's love.[9] Gaillardetz claims that we need focal practices and communal gatherings that disengage us from the isolated activities we immerse ourselves in and direct us to the goodness and beauty of creation.

A disengagement from the world of compulsive consumerism and engagement with the embodied world of God's presence demands a conscious decision to waste time among the ordinary and mundane. Modern technology's promise of immediacy, expediency and enjoyment lures us away from attentiveness, fidelity, perseverance and the ability to love others by spending time with them. We may no longer feel the world as God's creation because we no longer have to feel anything. Pleasure and pain are psychic opposites that we can now control at our leisure or set the limits of endurance. We live with a type of cultural anal-gesia, which extends from profound apathy and indifference to the denial of death. If the fundamental nature of human relationships is changing from an "I-Thou" relationship to an "I-It" relationship, then perhaps we are losing our ability to relate to others because we are los-ing our ability to love. When we fail to love, we fail to suffer the pain of others and thus we fail to live justly with compassion—for the poor, cre-ation and the world around us.

•

TRUE POVERTY

If the life of Francis holds out to us the need for conversion, as a turn-ing to the Earth and its people, such conversion must be the realization of our poverty as creatures. While the word "poverty" is a negative term that immediately connotes deprivation and dependency or perhaps a vow made by religious men and women, it is probably the most appro-priate word to describe the human condition. Poverty is rooted in the fact that we and creation ultimately do not control our existence. We come from God and belong to God. True poverty of being is not mate-rial deprivation or the sacrifice of life's essentials; rather, it is recognizing our need, and even more so, knowledge of our need, which renders us open, receptive and grateful. Poverty is an attitude of acknowledging that all is gift given to us by a God bending low in love. Those who are open and empty enough, who are in need to receive and to give forth what they have received, live in gratitude to God, and this gratitude is a spirit of conversion. Poverty is a virtue that belongs to all who are authentic persons, those who live in relationship and who can receive and respond to another. Those who are full of themselves, whether materially, emo-tionally or psychologically, are "sent away empty." The goodness of God's creation cannot be theirs, for they experience no need and therefore cannot receive. Only the truly poor can be rich because God fills one's emptiness. The poverty of created existence therefore reveals the rich-ness of divine presence. Poverty lends itself to interdependency, realizing that no one person is entirely self-sufficient, because every person is a creature of God. Francis rarely spoke of poverty in his writings, but when he did so, it was usually in the context of community: "Let each one love and care for his brother as a mother loves and cares for her son…"[10] Poverty humanizes us by making us dependent on one another, allowing us to care for another. By failing to live in the poverty of being, we indulge in a new form of self-assertion and pay the price for it: loneliness. Because we do not risk the poverty of openness, our lives are not graced with the warm fullness of human existence. We are left with only a shadow of our real self.

True poverty creates community because it converts self-sufficiency into creative interdependency where the mystery of life unfolds for us. Poverty can be our strength when our need is for love. Only those who can see and feel for another can love another. It is the same with creation. Only one who can taste the world renounces the spirit of possessing it. A life without possessing things *(sine proprio),* which is the heart of poverty for Francis, is a life of conversion that leads to community in creation. It is that free and open space within the human heart that welcomes the other person or creature of creation. Poverty, therefore, can nurture the grace of hospitality to creation. Hospitality does not seek to change others but to offer them a place to be, where strangers can enter and discover themselves as created free. Henri Nouwen claimed that we are so afraid of open spaces and empty spaces that we occupy them with our minds even before we are there.[11] Empty spaces reveal our intolerance of the incomprehensibility of people and events and make us look for labels or classification to fill the emptiness. Because empty space tends to create fear, we fill up our lives with "busyness," where being busy is a symbol of being alive.[12] Such preoccupations, Nouwen says, prevent us from having new experiences and keep us hanging onto familiar ways. How can we expect something really new to happen to us if our hearts and minds are so full of our own concerns that we do not listen to the sounds announcing a new reality? If we expect any salvation, redemption, healing and new life, the first thing we need is an open receptive place where something can happen to us. And this is the place of hospitality born of poverty, the open space where new life can flourish, where others can be welcomed, where hostility can be converted to friendship. We cannot change the world by a new plan, project or idea. We cannot change other people by our convictions, stories, advice and proposals, but we can offer a space where people are encouraged to disarm themselves, to lay aside their occupations and preoccupations and to listen with attention and care to the voices speaking in their own center.[13] In the same way, we can offer hospitality to creation, accepting creatures as they are, and allowing nature a space to be itself.

•

From Poverty to Justice

Conversion to poverty is conversion to justice, according to Bonaventure. Once we realize our need for God, we begin to realize our need for others including the created world itself. The grace of poverty is the grace of dependency, rendering us open and grateful for all that enables us to exist on this planet Earth. It is looking into the eyes of our neighbor and seeing there the light of God. It is touching the trees and the rocks and the Earth on which we stand and feeling there the goodness of God. It is standing with open arms in creation, knowing that in embracing the created world who nourishes us and sustains our lives, we embrace God. Justice is right relationship, respecting in others the inherent goodness that is uniquely theirs, and loving the good that is in them. It is granting to others what rightfully belongs to them as creatures of God and sharing with others what is ours to share. Justice is the sister of poverty because it acknowledges that nothing in this finite, earthly life truly belongs to any particular individual. Everything is contingent on the generosity of God and thus on the will of God. What we think we possess today may be taken away tomorrow. Only the truly poor live justly because they live without possessing anything and are willing to share everything.

The path to justice through poverty is guided by wisdom. Wisdom is knowledge deepened by love; it is a type of knowledge that filters through the heart of love. Wisdom, like justice, is the fruit of poverty. It is the heart open and free that can see the truth of things in their true being. In union with Christ crucified, Francis learned wisdom through the path of crucified love—by letting go into God, by accepting himself as a creature of God, by learning the art of sacrifice as essential to the deepening of love and by dying to the selfish self. By learning wisdom through the cross, Francis discovered that God's gracious love can never be outdone or effaced because it is the pulsating heart of the universe. In wisdom Francis found peace. Just as the power of God's love in the cross is the beginning of a new creation, Francis found that same love of wisdom at work in creation awaiting its new birth. Through the wisdom of the cross, Francis' life became transformative. Unafraid to sacrifice his own self for the sake of others, Francis challenged the unjust structures of his day by his solidarity with the poor and preached the gospel through his Christian life. Like Francis, we too are to build up in our own lives what is yet lacking in the Body of Christ. Francis shows us that only by surrendering ourselves to God and daring everything for love's sake, the Earth can be restored as our home and all creatures can become our brothers and sisters.

The true spirit of poverty that leads to justice must, by the very nature of radical interdependency, destabilize conversion as an individual endeavor and reorient it toward shared life in community. Poverty should lead us to confess our need for one another and for the Earth, to recognize that our lives are incomplete or rather nestled in sin, as long as we remain separate from one another and from the Earth. Conversion, therefore, is not an individual turning toward God; rather, it is turning to the Earth and thus to Earth's community of living things. The type of conversion needed today is not simply an enhancement of spirituality, as if we could say more prayers and try harder to be nice; rather, we need a type of "eco-penance," a turning to the Earth in a spirit of pardon, forgiveness, humility, charity and poverty. We need to relinquish our radical self-centered "I" and recognize our need for a "Thou." Conversion is engagement with the human *and* nonhuman world of amazing diversity and beauty; it is participation in creation's well-being. How can we turn from the trap of *Homo oeconomicus* to a new humanity of *Homo oikonomicus?* How do we overcome the modern sin of consumerism and renew the health of the Earth by finding ourselves integrated into the ecological web of life? Poverty and humility are the garments of the *Homo oikonomicus*. The one who can put on the spirit of poverty and humility and who can live interdependently in the web of life is the ecological human. Such a person who lives in openness to life in its many forms is one who is open to the Word of God in our midst, the Word that calls out: "Go, rebuild my *oikos,* which you can see is falling into ruin." We have a responsibility to God's Earth because it is the birthplace of our humanity; it is our mother. The commandment "honor your father and mother" must now also include the Earth: "Honor your mother, the Earth." For the Earth has made possible our lives and our salvation. Indeed, there is no salvation apart from the Earth.

We may find the need for conversion to Earth's community superfluous in view of consumerism's lure. But if we can envision a God-centered Earth rooted in poverty and justice, then we are already at the beginning of a life-giving conversion. The path of Francis can inspire us to become a new *Homo oikonomicus*. He heard the Word of God turning him from self-centeredness to God-centeredness, and he responded immediately: "This is what I want. This is what I desire!" The same Word of God speaks to us today: "Turn your minds and hearts to the Earth and you shall live." But what do we want? What do we desire? Francis desired God and the world around him was transformed in Christ. We too may desire God, but then we must desire all that is of God and that includes the Earth. All that we hope for in eternal life will not be attained apart from the Earth, for the Earth is God's creation, it is God's joy—and it must be our joy as well if we aim for God and for life in God.

NOTES

[1] Mary Beth Ingham, *Scotus for Dunces*, pp. 132–133; Kenan Osborne, "John Duns Scotus in the Postmodern Scientific World," *The Franciscan Intellectual Tradition*, Elise Saggau, trans. (St. Bonaventure, N.Y.: Franciscan Institute, 2003), pp. 57–82.

[2] This story is recounted in "The Little Flowers of Saint Francis," 21, in *FA:ED*, vol. 3, pp. 601–602.

[3] The word *releasement* is translated from the term *gelasenheit* coined by the great Dominican spiritual writer Meister Eckhart to describe a fundamental disposition, a "creative surrender to the mystery which works itself out in the brokenness and the healing, the agony and the joy of our lives." See Barbara Fiand, *Releasement: Spirituality for Ministry* (New York: Crossroad, 1987), p. xi.

[4] Fiand, p. 6.

[5] Ingham, p. 95.

[6] James Nash, "On the Subversive Virtue: Frugality," *Ethics of Consumption: The Good Life, Justice and Global Stewardship*, David A. Crocker and Toby Linden, eds., trans. (Lanham, Md.: Rowman and Littlefield, 1998), p. 421.

[7] Sallie McFague, *Life Abundant: Rethinking Theology and Economy for a Planet in Peril* (Minneapolis: Fortress, 2001), p. 75. Actually, McFague appropriates the term *Homo oeconomicus* from Max Oelschlaeger, *Caring for Creation: An Ecumenical Approach to the Environmental Crisis* (New Haven, Conn.: Yale University Press, 1994), p. 96.

[8] Kathleen Norris, *The Quotidian Mysteries: Laundry, Liturgy and "Women's Work"* (New York: Paulist, 1998), p. 10.

[9] Richard R. Gaillardetz, *Transforming Our Days: Spirituality, Community and Liturgy in a Technological Culture* (New York: Crossroad, 2000), p. 67.

[10] Francis of Assisi, "The Earlier Rule," IX.11, in *FA:ED*, vol. 1, p. 71.

[11] Henri J.M. Nouwen, *Reaching Out: The Three Movements of the Spiritual Life* (New York: Doubleday, 1975), p. 74.

[12] Nouwen, p. 73.

[13] Nouwen, p. 76.

[chapter twelve]

ECO-PENANCE—
CONVERSION IN ACTION

The fruit of conversion is a new way of acting in the world. However we must beware that action for action's sake does not have the power needed to bring about the sustainability revolution. Only action that flows from a converted heart—informed by contemplation, fueled by love and sustained in community—has the holding power to cocreate with God a new world that is just and sustainable for all, including all of God's creatures and future generations to come.

Once we begin to adopt Francis' worldview of our deep interrelatedness to all creation, and God incarnate in all living things, it is impossible to continue "business as usual." The world becomes for us what the leper was for Saint Francis—beloved kin. We connect and fall in love again with the world we were created for. When we love something as our own, taking action to protect it goes beyond mere duty—we are moved from the heart to safeguard and protect it in times of need. Living out of this kind of generous love for creation also roots us in the strength and resilience of that web of life, through the Spirit that connects it all. This strength in our connectedness is an important asset, because the more we deepen in love with our beautiful planet, the more likely we are beset by grief and pain at the suffering being inflicted on her.

This is where many of us stop and step off the challenging path of conversion. In order to continue to move from contemplation toward conversion, we must join with our loved ones and our communities of faith for support in approaching these painful realities with contemplative eyes—daring to see the reality of the situation, and encouraging each other to face rather than avoid the challenges. As we discussed in chapter nine, we must learn to glean the resources of our spiritual tradition to help us "sustain the gaze" and not lose heart. This type of contemplation within the context of community informs our actions—for both contemplation and action are required of an engaged spirituality.

If we can gather up all from within our spiritual tradition that gives us the strength and courage and continue down this path of conversion, it may well be "the grace that saves us" from destruction of our species and our home planet. It will take tremendous effort, but conversion has the power to help us "learn anew for the sake of the future."

For those readers who have by now heard the call, "Go, rebuild my *oikos*, my creation," this chapter can help you know how to boldly take action. The reflective actions discussed in this chapter are more challenging, but they also have a much larger potential impact on our world. These actions require us to adopt an "eco-penitential" stance in life—to transform our human way of living within the context of right relationship with creation. First, we are challenged to change our individual lifestyles, and then to invest time and energy to engage larger systems, such as our churches, and our economic and political institutions so that we can begin creating systems that reduce our impact on a much larger scale. The closing meditation reinforces and celebrates that our service to the world—our work of human hands—continues to bring God's incarnate love into our hurting world each day, despite the struggles we might face.

•

FOLLOWING THE FOOTPRINTS OF FRANCIS: SHRINKING OUR ECOLOGICAL FOOTPRINT

Our belief in the Incarnation can inspire us to take action to protect our world. Our God walked in creation as an incarnate being. Because Francis knew that creation was and continues to be the home of the

Incarnation, following in his footprints means looking seriously at the footprint *we* are leaving on creation. As Christians living in the United States, we cannot profess to follow Francis without seriously scrutinizing our five-planet ecological footprint. This American lifestyle conjures up images of a careless, burly giant walking our Earth, unaware of the enormous path of destruction trailing behind him. Contrast this with *il poverello,* the "little poor one" of Assisi, who walked barefoot over the land, rejoicing in all the beauty of the Earth's fragile beings, wearing one tunic and denouncing the wealth and status which society said was his birthright. For us Americans the path to following Francis simply cannot be taken without making radical lifestyle changes if we wish to do justice to Francis' message. Francis truly offers a model worthy of aspiring to in this time of needless waste and overconsumption.

On a finite planet, sustainability and equity are inseparably linked.[1] Knowing our own ecological footprint in an accessible, understandable way is the first step in shrinking our personal impact on the Earth and the poor and marginalized. Take as a starting point the average American footprint of twenty-four acres, and compare this to the footprints (in acres) of average citizens in Germany (10.9), Canada (18.5) and El Salvador (3.09).[2] Canadians and Western Europeans enjoy a standard of living comparable to ours in the United States, yet the average ecological footprint for Germany is half of ours!

1. Aim for a European lifestyle. What would it take for us, as followers of Francis in the United States, to cut our footprint in half—to live as close to a European lifestyle as we can? Are you aware of things you can do in the areas of energy, water, waste and purchasing that can reduce your ecological footprint? Resolve to spend time doing the research that is needed, and then choose one or two areas to focus on making needed changes. Two discussion courses are especially helpful in guiding groups through such concrete actions: *Choices for Sustainable Living* by Northwest Earth Institute,[3] and the *Eco-Team* program, available through the Empowerment Institute.[4] Francis reminds us to do this important work *in community*. Joining with friends or fellow parishioners can provide the support and accountability needed to take make lifestyle changes such as these.

2. Discern between "greed" and "need." Although it does not always feel as if we lead affluent lifestyles, this is often due to the fact that we are conditioned by our consumer society to "compare up" rather than to "compare down." There will always be someone richer than us, but when we compare the lifestyles we lead to the rest of the world, there is little doubt about our relative affluence. Take some time to reflect on your lifestyle choices. When you compare your lifestyle to others in our country and our world who are poorer than you, what excesses do you see? What ways can you simplify your life and thus be in solidarity with others in our world? Can you do this with an attitude of living a penitential life, rather than creating excessive guilt?

3. Plan ahead for large purchases. Oftentimes we do not plan ahead for new building or remodeling projects or making a larger purchase, because it takes more time or money to invest in more ecologically sound options. In this way, we again allow the values of convenience and thrift to dominate in our lives, rather than sustainability, community and justice. If we take the time to plan, and to save for any additional start-up costs, we can make ecologically sound choices, which will benefit us and creation for years to come. What "big ticket" items (cars, houses, remodeling projects, furnaces) are you considering buying in the next year? Would you be willing to do the research to determine the most ecologically sound purchase in this area?[5] What might you need to sacrifice in order to purchase in this way? Choose one area and take an intentional action to reduce your footprint.

4. Changing structures to reduce our collective impact. What would be required not only to reduce our American footprint to levels equivalent to other developed nations, but then to move *all* developed nations to a more just, equitable and sustainable footprint? Then, on a global level, we could find lasting ways to share the bounty of creation with all—humans and other living beings alike. Reflect as an individual or a group on one structural, societal or political change you can support to begin to transform our society to more equitable global consumption patterns. For example, you could take action to improve public transportation options in your town or city, to increase local food options, improve recycling programs, increase green energy options, lobby automobile makers to produce higher-efficiency vehicles, or urge local and state governments to require more ecologically sound decisions from businesses and government.

•

SHRINKING OUR INDIVIDUAL FOOD CONSUMPTION

We all know that our global economy has had a dramatic effect on where our food comes from, but many of us are unaware of the much larger ecological footprint that this creates. Currently, the average American meal travels 1,500 to 2,500 miles before it reaches our plate. This represents an increase of 25 percent in just twenty years.[6] We have become accustomed to something that no previous generation on Earth ever could have imagined: We eat as if it is summer year-round.[7] An unlimited choice of fresh fruits or vegetables come to our plates throughout the year, no matter how short the growing season in our part of the world. Consider the carbon footprint that this requires—for Americans to eat apples from New Zealand in the summer or bananas from South America any time of the year—to transport these items across hemispheres for our daily use (not to mention the fossil fuels which make the fertilizers used to grow them). It is now common practice to expend more energy (measured in food calories) to transport food than we gain from eating the food itself. For example, for every calorie of iceberg lettuce imported from California into England, 127 calories of nonrenewable fossil fuels were used to transport it.[8] Much of our inflated footprint is due to unnecessary excesses built into our current food system. FoodFirst reported that tomatoes for Heinz ketchup are grown in California, shipped to Canada to be bottled, and then sent back to be sold in California. A total of $431,000 worth of California almonds passed through New York City's port en route to Italy during the same year that $397,000 worth of imported Italian almonds passed through the same port into the United States. This kind of trade system, beset with mindless and excess waste, "mortgages our children's planet for profits today" as Kirsten Schwind, an expert on food trade, points out in her essay "Going Global on a Global Scale: Rethinking Food Trade in the Era of Clime Change, Dumping and Rural Poverty."[9]

Since 1920 Iowa has gone from producing most of its fruits and vegetables to importing them from afar. If Iowans committed to purchasing 10 percent more of their food from that grown within Iowa, they could collectively save 7.9 million pounds of carbon dioxide emissions annually. Eating food grown in our local bioregion is one action we can take that has a large positive impact on our ecological situation. Just what does "local" mean? Some who have embraced the task of eating locally have challenged themselves to eat only food grown within their county, others have limited the food they buy to a radius of a hundred miles from their home.[10] While this is a very difficult task to accomplish in today's global food system, taking the first steps toward eating locally can be quite illuminating. Since most American meals travel at least 1,500 miles from farm to plate, attempting to eat food grown within even 500 miles is challenging, but it can teach us more about eating with the season, challenge us to rediscover the lost arts of canning and preserving food, and help us discover local farmers and small companies within our own backyards worthy of supporting. Bill McKibben, author and commentator on Christianity and environmental issues, decided to take on the challenge of eating locally through the Vermont winter. He was interviewed in *National Geographic* about the experience:

> Last winter I conducted an experiment: Could I get through the cold months in my northern valley eating just the food grown in my county? As it turned out, I didn't simply survive; I thrived. There were plenty of

potatoes and onions and beets and beef and cider and beer and wheat and eggs, and just enough tomatoes canned in the heat of summer, to see me through. I'm sure I saved lots of energy, though I can't calculate just how much. What I can list, though, are the new friends I made, and they numbered in the dozens. My food cost more in terms of time; it wasn't as convenient to go to the farmer's market as to the Shop'n Save. But that cost, thought of differently, was actually the biggest benefit of the whole experiment.[11]

Although our current food system has been increasingly globalized, options for eating locally are increasing. Farmers' markets are growing in popularity, and their availability across the country has doubled in the last ten years.[12] Community supported agriculture (CSA) is another excellent option for eating locally. Through these small, member-supported farms, the Earth and the farmer are not treated as commodities, but as members of the community. Each growing season, shareholders pay a fixed rate and receive a certain quantity and variety of foods in return. Members share in the bounty of the harvest, but they also help the farmer shoulder risks posed by things such as weather and crop disease. Although it seems daunting at first to learn to prepare food that is local and in season, one can build one's repertoire over time to know how to cook with the harvest. A local farmer for a CSA farm helped his members in this task by offering recipes in his weekly newsletter and encouraging them to focus on learning a few recipes a month for one unfamiliar vegetable. Soon, cooking with each new and unfamiliar vegetable becomes second-nature, and it becomes easier the next month to move on to the next one. He called this practice "building virtue." (Thanks to Mark Boucher-Cobert for this insight.)

Eating locally can indeed help us build a virtuous life because it challenges us to grow individually and to build ties to our community, even as we build a healthier world for all of life and future generations. Eating locally is good for our health and the health of the planet, it is good for local farmers, it builds community, and it contributes significantly to curbing global warming. It is the perfect penitent action: requiring intention and sacrifice on the personal level, offering transformative potential on the societal level and in the meantime bringing into our lives many of the spiritual gifts that accompany the penitent life— simplicity, community, humility and joy.

1. Become mindful of your food purchasing patterns. Watch these patterns over a one-week or one-month period, without changing them. Begin to notice where your food comes from. What percentage of the food you normally purchase is grown locally?

2. Buy local for one month. For one month, select one area of your food purchasing (such as fruits and vegetables or dairy or meat) and purchase only locally grown food. Notice the sacrifices that this takes (choice, convenience) as well as the benefits it brings into your life.

3. Research local food sources. Spend one hour this week researching local food sources: farmers, farmers' markets, dairies. Consider purchasing food from them on a more regular basis.

•

SHRINKING OUR CHURCH'S FOOTPRINT

When Francis spoke about living out the virtue of poverty, he did so in the context of community. As we walk the path of conversion, we must also call our faith communities to join us in protecting creation. Bill McKibben issues a challenging call to Christians around the issue of global climate change: "…it's cause for celebration that we've reached this point [of increased awareness of the issue of climate change] with only modest contributions from the realms of business and religion. That means that there are reserves unspent in two crucial institutions."[13] He points out that the churches of our country could play a key role in discovering a "convivial environmentalism," one that goes beyond the grim work of trying to salvage the remnants of our dying Earth to one which "asks us to figure out what we really want out of life, [and] offers profound possibilities."[14] Churches, he says, are one of the places that see it as part of their purpose to articulate a vision for humanity that goes beyond the consumer ideal. They remind us that caring for each other and valuing the intangibles in life bring us deeper satisfaction.[15] Christians walking in the footsteps of Francis could help us fashion an environmental ethic that celebrates the recovery of the simple, authentic life and is not only about duty and responsibility but relationship, generosity and love.

Churches across the world have begun to make large-scale efforts to reduce their congregations' contributions to climate change and ecological problems. The Church of England has launched a denomination-wide "Shrinking Our Footprint" endeavor, challenging the entire church to accomplish "the forty-percent church"—creating a new church whose impact is 40 percent of its current levels. It suggests that all of its churches complete an energy audit and then begin a five-step path of change, which includes increasing energy efficiency, switching to green power and eventually generating their own power and offsetting any remaining carbon emissions.[16] They recognize how large-scale the changes will need to be to eventually reduce our carbon footprint in a way that will realistically avert climate change: a 60 to 70 percent reduction in carbon emissions in the next ten years. They respond to this recognition by daring to present a bold vision: "A wind turbine in a churchyard or PV cell installation on a church roof can make an iconic statement and be a visible symbol of the Church's commitment to adapting to climate change."[17]

In our own country Interfaith Power and Light has offered congregations assistance in performing energy audits, funding energy-reducing building upgrades and purchasing renewable power. St. Therese Catholic Church in Appleton, Wisconsin, was the 2004 Energy Star Congregation Award Winner for implementing church improvements that reduce energy and carbon emissions, saving the church 5,100 dollars per year and preventing 163,600 pounds of carbon dioxide emissions annually.

Reducing our ecological or carbon footprint on a church-wide level not only multiplies our positive impact, but it also engages others in action, increasing awareness and commitment to the crucial work of caring for creation together in our congregations. Join with others in your congregation to take action together, beginning with the actions suggested below:

1. Complete a church energy audit at your parish. The Regeneration Project's Interfaith Power and Light (IPL) campaign[18] is an interfaith ministry that helps faith communities "recognize and fulfill their responsibility for the stewardship of creation." There are IPL programs in twenty-four states, which offer assistance for helping congregations put their faith into action—emphasizing renewable energy, energy efficiency and conservation. They offer education for parishes, as well as energy audits and assistance in making a plan for implementing the recommendations. They also assist churches in large-scale energy projects such as rooftop solar energy and they encourage engagement by parishioners on a political level, advocating for sensible energy and global warming policy. Find out what is available from your state's IPL program and discuss what starting actions fit best in your parish. If your state does not have an IPL program, contact the national IPL campaign for assistance.

2. Implement a five-year action plan for reducing your parish's ecological impact. Using your energy audit as a baseline, set goals for increasing your parish's energy efficiency, conservation and recycling efforts, and decreasing its ecological or carbon footprint. Consider purchasing "green power" for all or a portion of your congregation's energy.[19] You can do this in more than thirty-five states through your regulated utility through "green pricing" programs, or you can purchase renewable energy certificates (RECs). Both programs send a message to power companies that increasing numbers of customers value investments in renewable energy sources.

3. Create a church transportation plan. Engage your church community in a dialogue about their travel to church services and other church activities. Establish neighborhood carpools, and offer recognition to parishioners for walking, biking, taking public transportation or carpooling to church. Through walking or biking to church, we can do more than curb our carbon emissions—we can reclaim the meaning of "Sabbath" by slowing down, simplifying our Sunday schedules, spending more time together as families, and getting to know parishioners in our own neighborhoods!

4. Create a church-wide effort to eat locally and support local farmers. Some parishes have offered to host local farmers' markets in their parking lots. Others purchase shares in a CSA and make the food available to members.[20] Initiate discussions on buying food locally. Host a "100-Mile" potluck, challenging participants to bring dishes made from local food and discuss religious implications of eating locally together. Earth Ministry offers the book *Food, Faith and Sustainability,* a reflection guide for faith communities on the topic of local food.[21]

5. Create a group to reflect and act on ecological issues. Consider inviting friends from your faith community to reflect on what God might be calling you to do as a group to care for creation. This might begin with actions mentioned in this chapter, such as measuring your ecological footprint and discussing ways to support each other in living more simple lifestyles.[22] Or, your group may decide to ask for more preaching and religious education programs about this issue. With a bit of determination, your group might find it worthwhile to address an environmental issue in your broader local community, such as habitat preservation, environmental education, sustainable building or public transportation. Any genuine progress in these areas will require engaging public officials and civic processes.

CHANGING OUR FOOTPRINT TO REFLECT A JUST WORLD

Rarely do our government and economic institutions lead the way when the needed changes are comprehensive and ask people to sacrifice and change their lifestyles. The urgency of our ecological crises makes it all the more critical that we remember this and not wait for governments to implement these changes. Eileen Claussen, President of the Pew Center on Global Climate Change, reminds us that the reason we have not made more progress on the ecological front is that we have not harnessed "the force of people—the sheer force of public pressure: Like the marketplace, government will deliver only if it perceives a demand. Only when we accept our responsibility and act on it—as citizens, as consumers, as investors—will government and the marketplace respond."[23] She suggests that we actively exercise our power as consumers, voters and investors to send a clear message that the opinion of the American public is changing and we demand products and policies that take the Earth into account.

This can be intimidating for anyone, especially at first. This is where people of faith must be able to draw on their greatest resources: prayer and community. Both of these were necessary for Francis to gather the courage to call others to conversion, but that is most certainly what he did. Our greatest contribution as people of faith may be articulating for each other why we should do this. As our culture continues to be ever-more gripped by greed, believers in the Creator of heaven and Earth will need to address the ethical dimension of environmental protection.

Living a simple lifestyle begins to restore justice in our world; when we truly live a penitent life in Francis' spirit of voluntary poverty, we build right relationships in our world. But until we bring the lived experience of our converted hearts into the larger world, we will not experience the fullness of the converted heart. We must not be content with transforming only our individual lives. We must, like Francis, find the courage to proclaim the transforming power of this good news to the world. If all Christians made the individual and church-wide changes we have discussed in this book, it would not be long before our elected officials would take notice. If each of us discerned our own unique talents and offered them to the cause of changing the direction of our society and healing our world, tremendous shifts would begin to happen. Together we would engage in the task of restoring right relationship in our world, and our grandchildren's children could look back on this time and thank us for participating in the sustainability revolution so that they, too, could share in the wondrous bounty of God's creation.

. . . .

GUIDED MEDITATION: HANDS OF SERVICE

This meditation can be used with faith groups to reinforce the larger purpose behind ecological and social service work they are doing together. Like our footprints, which leave behind a sign of God's incarnate presence in the world, our hands can provide a powerful symbol of how we can make an imprint of love and service on creation. This meditation was adapted from Joanna Macy's activity entitled "The Milling."[23]

Close your eyes, holding one of your hands in the other so that all your attention can go to the sensation of touch. Contemplate this hand of yours, this gift from God that we can so easily take for granted day after day. What is this object you are holding? There is life in it. If you were anywhere in outer space, in the furthest reaches of our galaxy, and you were to grasp that, you would know that you were home. It is only made here. This is a human hand of our planet Earth, and it brings unique and incredible gifts to the family of creation of which it is a part. Explore it with great curiosity as if you had never known one before, as if you were on a research mission from some other solar system. Flexing it, note the intricacy of the bone structure. Note the delicacy of the musculature, the soft, sensitive padding on palm and fingertips. No heavy shell or pelt encloses this hand. It is vulnerable; it is easy to break or burn or crush. It is an instrument of knowing as well as doing.

Now open your awareness to this hand's journey through this particular lifetime, ever since it opened like a flower as you came out of your mother's womb. Clever hand that has learned so much: learned to reach for breast or bottle, learned to tie shoes, learned to write and draw, learned to wipe tears, learned to give comfort and reassurance. Bring to your awareness the fact that there are people living now who believe they are worthwhile and lovable, because of what that hand has told them. There are people living now whose last touch in life will come from this hand, and they will be able to go into their dying knowing they are not abandoned. And there are people living now who will be healed in mind or body by the power that this hand allows to flow through it. So experience how much you want this hand to be strong and whole for this time, to serve its brother-sister beings and God's creation of which it is a part. Offer thanks for the incredible miracle of this hand, gifted to you and through which you can offer your gifts of service to the world. Offer a prayer for it to be strong and play its part in the building of a culture of sanity and decency and beauty.

This hand, too, connects you with all who have gone before, offering their hands in service to our world. Jesus, Francis, Clare and countless other saints—our cloud of witnesses—who loved the world and offered their lives to its service, and who turned to the beauty and comfort of creation to animate their faithful lives. Bring to mind your own cloud of witnesses, all those who inspire you to continue in your own path of service to our world. The same Spirit that moved through their lives moves now through yours and is made incarnate through the work of your human hands.

Now join hands with your neighbor. (If you are doing this

activity individually, picture holding hands with a circle of others who are engaged in this type of service in the world.) Reflect on the work you are doing to care for our sacred creation, both individually and in this community. No matter how big or small the action or intention, this circle of hands is doing the work of bringing about a healthy, life-sustaining world for all. But none of these hands can do it alone! We need community, we need support, we need people to remind us to engage our culture to make widespread change. We need people to give us space and permission to dare the darkness, to listen to the cry of the Earth and begin to usher in a life-giving society for all—rich and poor, human and nonhuman beings. These hands we hold remind us that our self does not stop at our own skin, but extends out to include this circle and the overlapping, interweaving circles of our families and extended communities. Our self expands to include Brother Sun and Sister Moon, Brother Wind and Sister Water, as well as all our brothers and sisters—the plants and trees and bugs and creatures. This circle of hands helps us remember the incredible gifts of being human as we walk daily in this world of wonder—the home of the Incarnation—even as we live amidst a society in which many people resist seeing this world as sacred.

The human mind, when unconscious and on autopilot, has proven to be one of the most destructive forces on this planet. But the conscious, intentional choices of the human mind with the converted heart have the power to build a new creation! The work of these human hands we each hold, geared toward service and fueled by love and compassion, can cocreate with God a new, life-sustaining society that will ensure a world for our grandchildren's children. Through this work, through these hands, we can join with our loving Creator and cocreate a world of beauty, justice and love. Amen.

- -

NOTES

[1] David Korten, *The Great Turning: From Empire to Earth Community,* from a lecture given in Portland, Oregon, May 2006.

[2] Global Footprint Network, "National Footprints," http://www.footprintnetwork.org.

[3] Northwest Earth Institute, *Choices for Sustainable Living,* trans. (Portland, Oreg.: NWEI, 2002).

[4] David Gershon and Andrea Barrist Stern, *Eco-Team: A Program Empowering Americans to Create Earth-Friendly Lifestyles* (New York: Empowerment Institute, 2003).

[5] See *Co-op America: Economic Action for a Just Planet.* It offers a "Responsible Shopper's Guide" and National Green Pages to help guide consumers in ecologically responsible purchasing and investing, http://www.coopamerica.org.

[6] Worldwatch Institute, "Globetrotting Food Will Travel Even Farther This Holiday Season," November 21, 2002; http://www.worldwatch.org.

[7] Bill McKibben, "A Grand Experiment: Living off the Land During a Long Vermont Winter Requires Patience, Planning, and a Little Help From Your Friends," *Gourmet,* July 2005.

[8] "Eating Oil: Food in a Changing Climate," A Sustain/Elm Farm Research Centre Report, December 2001; http://www.sustainweb.org/pdf/eatoil.

[9] Kirsten Schwind, "Going Local on a Global Scale: Rethinking Food Trade in the Era of Climate Change, Dumping and Rural Poverty" *Backgrounder,* Food First: Institute for Food and Development Policy, Spring/Summer, 2005.

[10] "100 Mile Diet: Local Eating For Global Change"; http://100milediet.org.

[11] Bill McKibben, "A Deeper Shade of Green," NationalGeographic.com; http://www7.nationalgeographic.com.

[12] McKibben, "A Deeper Shade of Green."

[13] McKibben, "Hot and Bothered: Facing up to Global Warming." *The Christian Century,* July 11, 2006, available from http://christiancentruy.org.

[14] McKibben, "Hot and Bothered: Facing Up to Global Warming."

[15] McKibben, "A Deeper Shade of Green."

[16] "Shrinking Our Footprint: The Church of England's National Environmental Campaign," http://www.shrinkingthefootprint.cofe.anglican.org.

[17] McKibben, "Hot and Bothered: Facing Up to Global Warming."

[18] The Regeneration Project, National Interfaith Power and Light Campaign; http://www.theregenerationproject.org.

[19] U.S. Department of Energy, Energy Efficiency and Renewable Energy/The Green Power Network, "Buying Green Power;" http://www.eere.energy.gov/greenpower/buying.

[20] National Catholic Rural Life Coalition, "What Can a Parish Do?" http://www.ncrlc.com/What-can-a-parish-do01.html.

[21] *Food, Faith and Sustainability: Environmental, Spiritual, Community and Social Justice Implications of the Gift of Daily Bread,* www.earthministry.org.

[22] To calculate your ecological footprint, take the "Ecological Footprint Quiz" www.redefiningprogress.org; or http://www.myfootprint.org.

[23] Eileen Claussen, "Climate Change: From Awareness to Action," PEW Center on Global Climate Change; http://www.pewclimate.org.

[24] Joanna Macy, *Coming Back to Life,* pp. 94–98.

[conclusion]

Scientists seldom agree on results unless the data is overwhelmingly convincing; thus, when a group of prize-winning scientists came together in 1990 to discuss the environment, their joint remarks, as we indicated in the introduction, were alarming. They declared that we are close to committing crimes against creation. "We are now threatened," they said, "by self-inflicted, swiftly moving environmental alterations about whose long-term biological and ecological consequences we are still painfully ignorant."[1] Although eighteen years have now passed since the scientists spoke out, things have not improved; indeed, they seem to have worsened. We are in a critical situation today. Scientists indicate that changes in global climactic systems and collapsing global biological diversity pose fundamental threats to the very future of human society. We are on the brink of humanitarian and ecological catastrophes; environmental disruption looms ominously.[2]

From a religious perspective, we are destroying modes of divine presence. For every species that is becoming extinct, the footprints of God are being irreversibly erased. We are, by our own will and hubris, degrading the good Earth given to us as a gift by the divine Giver. To degrade the Earth is to interfere with the message of its Creator; it is a way of rejecting God by rejecting God's self-expression, as God communicates himself to us in the diversity of creation. The Franciscan diagnosis on the environmental crisis is a broken relationship between God and creation. The mirror of creation has been shattered. What remains of the shattered mirror of creation is the unbridled human will to power, the irrepressible human urge to be gods. Do Christians have a responsibility for this shattered mirror of creation? Yes, simply because we claim to be incarnational people and have failed to live the truth of the Incarnation, that God dwells among us in persons, creatures and all living beings in creation. If we do not speak out for creation, we condone the violence against creation and hence vindicate the prejudice against the Incarnation. We resist the truth of the claim that the Word is made flesh. If we reject belief in this Earth as the cosmic nature of Christ, then we must admit we are crucifying Christ not simply by crucifying one another but by crucifying the body of the Earth.

If conversion is necessary to turn (or return) to the Earth, then we need a conversion to the Incarnation. We must reclaim Jesus Christ as the center and meaning of our lives—our identity. Herein may be the most difficult task because such conversion requires personal, communal and institutional commitment. A return to the Incarnation does not simply mean a narrow-minded exclusive truth claim that Jesus saves; rather, it means *living* in relation to the Earth as the Body of Christ. Francis' *Canticle of the Creatures* never once mentions the name of Jesus Christ; yet, the entire hymn is filled with the mystery of Christ. So, too, must be our lives if we are to be "Christ-bearers," giving witness to the good news of God among us.

The insights of the Franciscan tradition can help us understand why living in the Incarnation, the risen and glorified Christ, is valuable to the healing of the Earth. From the life of Francis we affirm the overflowing goodness of the triune God as the source of creation. Creation is not on the fringe of divine power but flows out of the heart of an infinitely loving Creator. As a limited actualization of the infinite self-diffusive good, creation is caught up in the mystery of the generation of the Word from the Father. God speaks to us in the book of creation, and this "God-talk" renders all creation holy; all is sacrament. The intrinsic relationship between creation and the Incarnation means that the God who creates is the God who saves; indeed, only by living in Christ does the new creation unfold. In Scotus's view it is the primacy of Christ that imparts an inherent dignity to everything that exists in creation, and he develops this idea through his doctrine of individuation or *haecceitas*. Everything in its unique being, its "thisness," speaks of Christ because every aspect of creation is related to Christ, who is the pattern of the universe. Both Bonaventure and Scotus emphasize that Christ is the head of creation, the first in God's intention to love. The whole creation is made for Christ who is its source and goal. It is Christ who opens our eyes to the goodness of creation by which we come to see the divinity hidden in ordinary, created reality. The whole creation is charged with the grandeur of God and we are called to see and to love this gracious goodness in the everyday beauty of creation. As book and mirror, creation both proclaims God from within and reflects God. To stand in creation as the sacrament of God is to stand in mystery. The richness of God's love provides a basis for explaining the richness and diversity of the created world. God is the mystery of self-diffusive love that is beyond measure. If the world is, in some way, an external expression of that mystery, and if no single created word can give adequate expression to the richness of that mystery, it is not surprising that there is a rich variety in creation through which the eternal mystery of love finds expression. As Bonaventure realized, the created order is a rich symbol that mediates to us the simplicity and richness of God.

The life of Francis speaks to us clearly of Christian life in the gift of creation. The ideals of brotherhood, sisterhood, piety and family all connote a peaceful coexistence of cooperation and mutual dependence. But the life of Francis also holds out for us an essential point. We are, as Philip Hefner claimed, created cocreators, created to help bring about the new creation on this Earth.[3] Bonaventure, too, realized that the Body of Christ (which includes the Earth) is incomplete and can only be completed by those who live in relation to this Body as a living Body. We humans stand in a unique position between God and the nonhuman world, which longs for its completion in God. The fundamental relationship between Incarnation and creation leads to the idea that each and every aspect of creation has absolute dignity because everything is created specifically and uniquely through the Word of God. We humans are related to the nonhuman things of creation because we are intimately related to the Word of God. "Are we willing to bear the interdependence and responsiveness of the God-reality in the wombs of our being for the good of this world?"[4] Without a life of conversion supported by poverty and prayer, brotherhood and sisterhood in creation is absurd. Without the human voice to give God glory in the beauty of creation, without human eyes to see the divine splendor hidden in creation, and without the human heart to love that beckons to be loved, creation is mute; it is lifeless and the object of selfish power. Bonaventure reminds us that if we fail to perceive our vocation as Christians, we bear the revolt that awaits us. He wrote:

> Therefore any person who is not illumined by such great splendor in created things is blind. Anyone who is not awakened by such great outcries is deaf. Anyone who is not led by such effects to give praise to God is mute. Anyone who does not turn to the First Principle as a result of such signs is a fool. Therefore open your eyes; alert your spiritual ears; unlock your lips, and apply your heart so that in all creatures you may see, hear, praise, love, and adore, magnify, and honor your God lest the entire world rise up against you.[5]

Such words raise the question, what is ours to do? How should we relate to creation? How can we understand the human journey to God as one that includes creation? How can the tradition help us overcome violence to creation and restore relationships of peace and justice? Is it enough simply to "recycle" or "turn off the lights" or does our tradition call us to a more radical stance with regard to creation? Here are some points to consider:

- We must realize our interconnectedness to creation. Part of our poverty is to realize our dependency on the things of the created world. The Franciscan tradition offers the familial model of relating to creation left to us by Francis. Franciscan spirituality means changing our internal focus or consciousness. A new consciousness must call us to an active stance as "brother" and "sister" to the nonhuman creation.

- Developing a new Franciscan consciousness also means an awareness of the intrinsic value of everything that exists. We need to pay attention to the details of creation, perhaps striving for a contemplative gazing on nature. To gaze into things is a way of seeing Christ.

- Following the Franciscan emphasis on a Christ-centered universe, contact with nature needs to be a fundamental component of our Franciscan way of life. A trip to the ocean, a walk in the woods, working in the garden are important not primarily for what they produce, but for their inherent Christ-contact. As Hopkins wrote to a friend, "I think that the trivialness of life is, and personally to each one ought to be seen to be, done away with by the Incarnation."[6]

- We must come to realize that our sinful actions are at the root of our present ecological crisis and thus our need for ongoing penance or conversion. The Franciscan practice of penance embodies humility. It consists in acknowledging our brokenness and sinfulness. The practice of "Eco-penance" is both an interior attitude and a praxis. It can promote consistency between the statement of values we make about creation and our behavior toward it.

- Believing in the inherent goodness of creation and the dignity of each created thing should lead to a stance on environmental justice. Justice entails right and loving relationships and thus a stance to oppose or change relationships that exploit the poor or cause environmental hazards to the poor.

- Awareness of biological diversity as an expression of the goodness of God means addressing the interdependence of the many forms of life on our planet. It is realizing that injury or extinction of one species can affect an entire ecosystem, indeed our very selves, because our relationship with creation is of complete interdependence.

- Preaching and living simplicity of life are profoundly countercultural acts in capitalistic America. A contemporary Franciscan spirituality of creation must be based on learning to live with expressions of voluntary poverty out of love for the Earth and the poor and to find great joy in this simplicity. This modern world is a cacophony of competing demands for our money. Can we find the freedom to live in simpler houses with smaller cars and fewer toys?

- The sustainability revolution will not take place until people demand it of public decision makers. We must find ways to bring this Franciscan perspective to the marketplace of ideas. Many elected officials are, in fact, quite intrigued by the expression of religious and spiritual values that pertain to the common good. We have to find a way to speak to public officials with the same courage as Francis had. Creation cannot vote in elections and so it is waiting for us to speak on its behalf.

- We should find ways of engaging scientists in dialogue. Many of them are deeply concerned about the future of the human enterprise on this planet, but few know how to find communities of ethical concern. Many fundamentalist religious leaders in America are expressing disdain for science and outright condemnation of scientists. A Franciscan approach seeks to build bridges with all people of good will. A public partnership between scientists and committed followers of Jesus to speak on behalf of the Earth cannot be ignored.

- We must pray for creation and for the conversion of human hearts so that we treat our Sister Mother Earth, with the kindness and respect she deserves.

Finally, it is helpful to realize that we live in an evolutionary universe with *Christ as the center and goal*. To be Franciscans in an evolutionary universe is to have an awareness that our actions have the power to help move the universe toward its fulfillment in Christ, or they may thwart this goal. What we do matters to the matter of the universe. Francis' love for creation led him to realize that the world will not be destroyed. It will be brought to the conclusion which God intends for it from the beginning. And that beginning is anticipated in the mystery of the incarnate Word and the glorified Christ. With Christ, all the lines of energy in the universe are coordinated and unified; all comes together in unity and coherence; and all is finally brought to its destiny with God.[7]

NOTES

[1] David Toolan, *At Home in the Cosmos*, p. 9.

[2] Keith Douglass Warner, "Taking Nature Seriously: Nature Mysticism, Environmental Advocacy and the Franciscan Tradition," in *Franciscans and Creation: What is Our Responsibility?* Elise Saggau, ed. (St. Bonaventure, N.Y.: Franciscan Institute, 2003), p. 55.

[3] See *The Human Factor: Evolution, Culture and Religion* (Minneapolis.: Fortress, 1993), pp. 23–51. Hefner writes: "Human beings are God's created co-creators whose purpose is to be the agency, acting in freedom, to birth the future that is most wholesome for the nature that has birthed us—the nature that is not only our own genetic heritage, but also the entire human community and the evolutionary and ecological reality in which and to which we belong. Exercising this agency is said to be God's will for humans," p. 27.

[4] Renate Craine, *Hildegard: Prophet of the Cosmic Christ* (New York: Crossroad, 1998), p. 77.

[5] Bonaventure, *Itinerarium Mentis in Deum* 1.15. Zachary Hayes, trans. *Itinerarium Mentis in Deum* in *Works of St. Bonaventure*, vol. 2, P. Boehner and Z. Hayes, eds. (St. Bonaventure, N.Y.: Franciscan Institute, 2002), p. 61.

[6] Short, "Pied Beauty," p. 35.

[7] Hayes, "Christ, Word of God and Exemplar," p. 13.

APPENDIX A

USING THE METHOD OF REFLECTIVE ACTION

A variety of activities are offered in the reflective action chapters to inspire creative ways to integrate the concepts of this book. It is not enough to *know* the concepts introduced in this book—most of us already have most of the information we need. What is needed, as Francis would say, are hearts ignited by love. Therefore, this book offers spiritual practices, individual and group activities and practical actions that can be taken into the reader's own life to truly begin to live an engaged Franciscan spirituality. Because of this, the reflective action chapters will not read in the same way as the other chapters. It is best to choose the one or two activities that attract you the most, and then take your time with them. Take them into your prayer life, and find small ways to incorporate them in whatever way fits for you. This will allow you to truly integrate the content of the entire section into your spiritual life. You may decide to practice one activity for a while, and then return to other suggested activities when you are ready to further deepen your experience of that section's topic. We encourage you to adapt these activities to suit your personal or local needs. Depending on where you live, what season it may be or your life circumstances, adapt the activity in a way that will enhance you or your group's ability to enter into the activity most fully.

Some of these activities may require you to do things that at first feel new and unfamiliar. We encourage you to approach these with a "beginner's mind," using Francis' delightful sense of wonder as a guide. Whenever possible, it is helpful to do these activities outside, surrounded by the magnificence of creation. Enjoy the experience of walking with Francis! Allow him to companion you on the critical journey of learning to care for God's gift of creation. As we Christians seek ways to address our present-day ecological challenges, Saint Francis can teach us how to do so with faith and love.

APPENDIX B

PREPARING FOR GUIDED PRAYER EXPERIENCES

Guided prayers and meditations are a powerful way to enhance your prayer life, whether they are done personally or in the context of a faith-based group. If you are bringing them into your personal prayer, initially it is best to follow the steps below, until you become familiar enough with the meditation to become more flexible with its use. If you are using the guided meditation within the context of a group meeting, you can have one person read it while the rest of the group listens, but otherwise the same guidelines apply.

Find a comfortable place where you can relax for about fifteen to thirty minutes. Make sure this place is free from distractions: Unplug the phone or turn off your cell phone, let your family or housemates know that you would like to be undisturbed and for how long. It is also important to choose a time of day when you are awake and alert. You may want to light a candle or some incense as a sensory reminder that this is sacred time. Give yourself the gift of stillness—time to be in the presence of God with Saint Francis as your guide.

You may choose to read the meditations offered in this book one paragraph at a time, closing your eyes between readings, and allowing your imagination and intention to enter into the prayer experience. Or it may be less distracting to make a recording of you or a friend slowly and quietly reading the meditation aloud. (If you decide to use a recording, be sure that the reader pauses long enough to let the listener's imagination fully consider the suggestions.)

During the guided prayer, you may notice your mind wandering away from the experience. This can be very frustrating, but know that it is quite common. Our minds are active all day and do not quickly make the transition between normal daily activity and sacred time. Meditation and prayer experiences help us become more skilled at noticing and redirecting our mind's movements so that our well-being is not as much at its mercy. With practice, we can learn to harness our mind to enhance, not distract from, our prayer experiences. We can borrow from our Catholic tradition of centering prayer, which offers us helpful tools in order to do this. When you notice that your mind has drifted, gently and *without judgment* simply label what is happening ("thinking," "worrying," "planning") and then redirect your attention back to your breath or a sacred word or phrase you have chosen. Set an intention to redirect your attention and surrender to God's presence. It is important to remember with centering prayer and guided meditation that it is the *process,* not the *results* that matter. The measure of "success" is *not* in controlling your mind perfectly! Instead, think of it as exercising a muscle: Each time you redirect your attention, you are strengthening the mind's ability to be mindful and "reaffirming your intention to consent to God's presence and action within." This, in turn, will enhance your prayer experience and your ability to be present to the sacred in your daily life.

APPENDIX C

CALCULATING YOUR INDIVIDUAL CARBON EMISSIONS

Calculate a measure of your personal or household carbon emissions at one of these online carbon calculators, or use the written one following, provided by Climate Solutions:

U.S. Environmental Protection Agency Global Warming Resource Center, Personal Greenhouse Calculator
http://www.epa.gov/climatechange/emissions/ind_calculator.html

Bonneville Environmental Foundation
https://www.greentagsusa.org/GreenTags/calculator_intro.cfm

Carbon Neutral Company
http://www.carbonneutral.com/uscalculator/index.asp

Climate Care
http://www.climatecare.org

*For a customized estimate of your household's CO_2 output,
use the following formula:*

	(Units x Conversion factor = total)
1. Estimate gallons of gasoline purchased per month. (From last month's gasoline receipts or number of miles driven monthly divided by your car's miles per gallon.)	____ gallons x 20 = ____ lbs. CO_2
2. Find your electricity bill from April or October (as an average for the year) and find kWh used or gather your electricity bills for the year and divide by 12.	____ kWh x 1 = ____ lbs. CO_2
3. If you use natural gas, find your April or October bill (as an average) and find how many therms you used.	____ therms x 12 = ____ lbs. CO_2
4. If you use heating oil, estimate total gallons purchased per year and divide by 12.	____ therms x 12 = ____ lbs. CO_2

Monthly CO_2 emissions from household = _____ x 12 = _____ lbs of CO_2
(Annual CO_2 emissions from household)

Climate Solutions

Main Office:

219 Legion Way SW, Suite 201, Olympia, WA 98501-1113

Phone: 360-352-1763; Fax: 360-943-4977

E-mail: info@climatesolutions.org

Seattle Office/Northwest Climate Connections:

1601 2nd Ave., Suite 615, Seattle, WA 98101

Phone: 206-443-9570; Fax: 206-728-0552

[select bibliography and resources]

ENVIRONMENTAL STUDIES BOOKS

Carroll, John E, and Keith Warner, eds. *Ecology and Religion: Scientists Speak*. Quincy, Ill.: Franciscan, 1998.

Speth, James Gustave. *Red Sky at Morning: America and the Crisis of the Global Environment*. New Haven, Conn.: Yale University Press, 2004.

Suzuki, David and Amanda McConnell. *Sacred Balance: Rediscovering Our Place in Nature*. Vancouver, B.C.: Greystone, 1997.

Uhl, Christopher, *Developing Ecological Consciousness: Pathways to a Sustainable World*. Lanham, Md.: Rowman and Littlefield, 2004.

Wilson, Edward O. *The Future of Life*. New York: Vintage, 2002.

—————. *The Creation: An Appeal to Save Life on Earth*. New York: W.W. Norton, 2006.

•

BOOKS ON FRANCISCAN THEOLOGY AND SPIRITUALITY

Allen, Paul M., and Joan deRis Allen. *Francis of Assisi's Canticle of the Creatures: A Modern Spiritual Path*. New York: Continuum, 1996.

Armstrong, E.A. *St. Francis: Nature Mystic. The Derivation and Significance of the Nature Stories in the Franciscan Legends*. Berkeley, Calif.: University of California Press, 1973.

Boff, Leonardo. *Cry of the Earth, Cry of the Poor*. New York: Orbis, 1997.

Delio, Ilia. *A Franciscan View of Creation: Learning to Live in a Sacramental World*, Elise Saggau, ed., vol. 2, *The Franciscan Heritage Series*, Joseph P. Chinnici, ed. St. Bonaventure, N.Y.: Franciscan Institute, 2003.

—————. *Franciscans and Creation: What Is Our Responsibility?* Elise Saggau, ed. St. Bonaventure, N.Y.: Franciscan Institute, 2004.

Doyle, Eric. *St. Francis and the Song of Brotherhood and Sisterhood*. St. Bonaventure, N.Y.: Franciscan Institute, 1997.

Ethics of Consumption: The Good Life, Justice and Global Stewardship. David A. Crocker and Toby Linden, eds. Lanham, Md.: Rowman and Littlefield, 1998.

Ingham, Mary Beth. *Scotus for Dunces: A Simple Guide to the Subtle Doctor.* St. Bonaventure, N.Y.: Franciscan Institute, 2003.

McFague, Sallie. *Life Abundant: Rethinking Theology and Economy for a Planet in Peril.* Minneapolis: Fortress, 2001.

Nothwehr, Dawn M., ed. *Franciscan Theology of the Environment: An Introductory Reader.* Quincy, Ill.: Franciscan, 2003.

Sorrell, Roger D. *St. Francis of Assisi and Nature: Tradition and Innovation in Western Christian Attitudes toward the Environment.* New York: Oxford University Press, 1988.

Toolan, David. *At Home in the Cosmos.* Maryknoll, N.Y.: Orbis, 2003.

•

BOOKS ON ECOLOGICAL SPIRITUALITY AND REFLECTIVE ACTION

Berry, Thomas. *The Great Work: Our Way Into the Future.* New York: Bell Tower, 1999.

Dowd, Michael. *EarthSpirit: A Handbook for Nurturing an Ecological Christianity, Third ed.* New London, Conn.: Twenty-Third, 1992.

Macy, Joanna, and Molly Young Brown. *Coming Back to Life: Practices to Reconnect Our Lives, Our World.* Gabriola Island, B.C.: New Society, 1998.

Palmer, Parker. *The Active Life: A Spirituality of Work, Creativity, and Caring.* San Francisco: Jossey-Bass, 1990.

Swimme, Brian. *Hidden Heart of the Cosmos: Humanity and the New Story.* New York: Orbis, 1996.

•

VIDEO RESOURCES FOR SPIRITUALITY AND SUSTAINABILITY

An Inconvenient Truth. 2006. Directed by Davis Guggenheim.

The Next Industrial Revolution. 2003. Produced by Shelly Morhaim.

The Work That Reconnects. 2007. Training DVD about the work of Joanna Macy. New Society Publishers.

Thomas Berry: The Great Story. 2002. Produced by Nancy Stetson and Penny Morrell.

WEB SITES AND RESOURCES FOR REFLECTIVE ACTION
Center for a New American Dream, 6930 Carroll Ave., Suite 900,
Takoma Park, MD 20912; http://www.newdream.org/; 301-891-3683
or 877-68-DREAM, provides resources and programs to help
Americans consume responsibly to protect the environment, enhance
quality of life and promote social justice.

Climate Solutions: Practical Solutions to Global Warming, 219 Legion
Way SW, Suite 201, Olympia, WA 98501-1113, is a nonprofit organization offering education and creative programming to help people act to
reduce global warming; http//www.climatesolutions.org; 360-352-1763
or 206-443-9570.

Co-op America: Economic Action for a Just Planet, 1612 K Street NW,
Suite 600, Washington DC 20006, offers helpful resources for responsible shopping, social investing, green business practices, climate change,
fair trade, green energy and more; http://www.coopamerica.org/; 800-
584-7336.

Earth Ministry, 6512 23rd Ave. NW, Suite 317, Seattle WA 98117, provides discussion courses, videos and resources for congregations in the
area of care for creation; 206-632-2426; http://www.earthministry.org/.

Empowerment Institute, P.O. Box 428, Woodstock, NY 12498, provides
empowerment tools aimed at creating measurable behavior change on
the individual, organizational and community levels, 845-657-7788,
http://www.empowermentinstitute.net/.

Northwest Earth Institute, 317 SW Alder, Suite 1050, Portland, OR
97204, provides discussion groups such as *Voluntary Simplicity, Deep
Ecology, Choices for Sustainable Living, Developing a Sense of Place, Healthy
Children Healthy Planet, Globalization and Its Critics* and *Global Warming,
Changing Course*. These courses are offered across the United States
through affiliated sister institutes; 503-227-2807; http://www.nwei.org/.

The Regeneration Project, National Interfaith Power and Light Campaign, P.O. Box 29336, The Presidio, San Francisco, CA 94129, provides support and assistance to faith congregations in areas of renewable energy, energy efficiency and conservation; 415-561-4891.

[index]

See also agriculture

Forum on Religion and Ecology, 14

fossil fuels, burning, 29

Francis, Saint

  addressing social ills, 167

  books on theology and spirituality of, 213–214

  conversion of. *See* conversion, of Francis

  cosmos of, 12–13, 36–37

  and deference toward all nature, 86–87

  early years, 38–39

  as first ecologist, 38–41

  heart of, 125–126

  and humble approach to creation, 77–79

  and lepers, 49, 140–141

  and living Word of God, 11–12

  as patron saint of ecology, 8–9

  as peacemaker, 88–89

  as prayer personified, 124–125

  and rebuilding *oikos*, 145–152

  and wolf of Gubbio, 172

"A Franciscan Ecological Examination of Conscience," 95, 99–101

Gaillardetz, Richard, 50

Genesis, and human responsibility over creation, 75

global climate, disruption in, 118–120

global climate change

  and contemplative prayer, 15

  effects in various regions, 118–119

  how to stop, 120–122

  impact on habitats, 73

  scientific evidence and opinion on, 119–120

  understanding, 111–116

  See also greenhouse gases

God

  and creation as "God-talk," 202–203

  identity in, 52

  world "pregnant with," 130–132

Golden Rule, as ethical approach to environmentalism, 74–77

greed

  American consumption as, 162, 164

  versus need, 188

greenhouse gases, 116–118

"greening of religion," 74

group activity, "Listening to the Plight of Our Sister, Mother Earth," 104–107

group reflection, to rebuild *oikos*, 147–152

guided meditation

  breathing through, 142–144